INSTRUCTOR'S EDITION

THE BIG PICTURE

READINGS FOR DEVELOPING WRITERS

INSTRUCTOR'S EDITION

THE BIG PICTURE
READINGS FOR DEVELOPING WRITERS

Jill A. Lahnstein

Cape Fear Community College

Upper Saddle River, New Jersey 07458

Editor in Chief: Leah Jewell
Senior Aquisitions Editor: Craig Campanella
Production Editor: Kathleen Sleys
Prepress and Manufacturing Buyer: Ben Smith
Marketing Manager: Rachel Falk
Marketing Assistant: Christine Moodie
Cover Design: Kiwi Design
Cover Director: Jayne Conte
Cover Art: Daryl Benson, photographer/Masterfile Corp.

This book was set in 11/13 Bembo by ElectraGraphics, Inc.,
and was printed and bound by Courier Companies, Inc.
The cover was printed by Coral Graphics, Inc.

© 2003 by Pearson Education, Inc.
Upper Saddle River, New Jersey 07458

For permission to use copyrighted material, grateful acknowledgment
is made to the copyright holders listed on pages 224–225, which are
considered an extension of this copyright page.

Printed in the United States of America
10 9 8 7 6 5 4 3 2 1

ISBN 0-13-093835-1 (student edition)
ISBN 0-13-093836-X (instructor's edition)

Pearson Education LTD., London
Pearson Education Australia PTY, Limited, Sydney
Pearson Education Singapore, Pte. Ltd
Pearson Education North Asia Ltd, Hong Kong
Pearson Education Canada, Ltd, Toronto
Pearson Educación de Mexico, S.A. de C.V.
Pearson Education—Japan, Tokyo
Pearson Education Malaysia, Pte. Ltd
Pearson Education, Upper Saddle River, New Jersey

Contents

Preface   xii

Unit I: People 1

An Indian Father's Plea: Don't Label My Son a "Slow Learner" (LETTER) ~ ROBERT LAKE   2

The Good Daughter (ESSAY) ~ CAROLINE HWANG   9

Dead Man Walking (BOOK EXCERPT) ~ SISTER HELEN PREJEAN   13

Reflections (ESSAY) ~ KENNY JACKSON   18

Girl (SHORT STORY) ~ JAMAICA KINCAID   23

The Shakers
The Mystical World of the Shakers (TEXTBOOK EXCERPTS) ~
JAMES HENRETTA, DAVID BRODY, SUSAN WARE,
AND MARILYNN S. JOHNSON   26

Mother to Son (POEM) ~ LANGSTON HUGHES   31

The New Testament (BOOK EXCERPT) ~ JAMES MCBRIDE   33

Suggestions   38
Profiling People   40

Unit II: Places 41

Po Folks: Off with Their Heads (SHORT STORY) ~
MARGO WILLIAMS   42

Is There Life on Mars? (TEXTBOOK EXCERPT) ~
TERESA AND GERALD AUDESIRK   47

Along the Tortilla Curtain (ESSAY) ~ PETE HAMILL   50

A Fable for Tomorrow (BOOK EXCERPT) ~ RACHEL CARSON   55

In the Suburbs (POEM) ~ LOUIS SIMPSON   59

The House on Mango Street (NOVEL EXCERPT) ~
SANDRA CISNEROS   61

What We Can Learn from Japan's Prisons (ESSAY) ~
JAMES WEBB **64**

Familiar Footing (ESSAY) ~ CHERYL SABA **71**

Suggestions 75

Profiling Places 76

Unit III: Events 77

Taunting of a Suicidal Woman Shocks Seattle (NEWSPAPER ARTICLE) ~
PATRICK MCMAHON **78**

Dreaming: Mysterious Mental Activity During Sleep (TEXTBOOK
EXCERPT) ~ SAMUEL L. WOOD AND ELLEN GREEN WOOD **81**

Last Flight (LETTER) ~ ISAO MATSUO **88**

Because I could not stop for Death (POEM) ~ EMILY
DICKINSON **91**

Body Ritual among the Nacirema (ESSAY) ~ HORACE MINER **93**

38 Who Saw Murder Didn't Call Police (ESSAY) ~ MARTIN
GANSBERG **99**

Growing Up Game (ESSAY) ~ BRENDA PETERSON **104**

The Story of an Hour (SHORT STORY) ~ KATE CHOPIN **109**

Suggestions 113

Profiling Events 114

Unit IV: Phenomena 115

Looking Up At Something (POEM) ~ DENNIS SAMPSON **116**

Now Hear This: Shhhhhhhhh (ESSAY) ~ JEANETTE BATZ **119**

Hooked on Anger (ESSAY) ~ RUSSELL BAKER **124**

The Tell-Tale Heart (SHORT STORY) ~ EDGAR ALLAN POE **127**

The Right Chemistry (ESSAY) ~ ANASTASIA TOUFEXIS **133**

Health Watch: Eating Disorders—Betrayal of the Body (TEXTBOOK
EXCERPT) ~ TERESA AND GERALD AUDESIRK **139**

Fear Not (ESSAY) ~ JEFFREY KLUGER **142**

Childless . . . with Children (ESSAY) ~ ANDY STEINER **151**

Suggestions 155

Profiling Phenomena 156

Unit V: Issues 157

What Is Poverty? (SPEECH) ~ JO GOODWIN PARKER   158

A Valuable Tapestry (RADIO BROADCAST) ~
SHIRLEY HART BERRY   **164**

In Praise of the F Word (ESSAY) ~ MARY SHERRY   167

The Hammer Man (SHORT STORY) ~ TONI CADE BAMBARA   171

The Powwow at the End of the World (POEM) ~
SHERMAN ALEXIE   **179**

*A Dose of Reality:The Truth about North America's Greatest
Drug Problem. Ritalin.* (ESSAY) ~ RICHARD DEGRANDPRE   182

Racism and Sexism in the Media (TEXTBOOK EXCERPT) ~
MARGARET ANDERSEN AND HOWARD F. TAYLOR   **186**

To Pet or Not to Pet? (ESSAY) ~ NADYA LABI   192

Suggestions   196

Profiling Issues   198

Appendix I: Context Clues   200

Appendix II: Word Parts   203

Appendix III: Summary Writing   207

Appendix IV: Characteristics of Effective Writing   210

Appendix V: The Writing Process   219

Credits   223

Instructor's Manual   IM-1

Rhetorical Contents

Narration

The Good Daughter (ESSAY) ~ CAROLINE HWANG   **9**

Dead Man Walking (BOOK EXCERPT) ~ SISTER HELEN PREJEAN   **13**

Reflections (ESSAY) ~ KENNY JACKSON   **18**

The Shakers
The Mystical World of the Shakers (TEXTBOOK EXCERPTS) ~
JAMES HENRETTA, DAVID BRODY, SUSAN WARE,
AND MARILYNN S. JOHNSON   **26**

The New Testament (BOOK EXCERPT) ~ JAMES MCBRIDE   **33**

Po Folks: Off with Their Heads (SHORT STORY) ~
MARGO WILLIAMS   **42**

Along the Tortilla Curtain (ESSAY) ~ PETE HAMILL   **50**

The House on Mango Street (NOVEL EXCERPT) ~
SANDRA CISNEROS   **61**

Familiar Footing (ESSAY) ~ CHERYL SABA   **71**

Taunting of a Suicidal Woman Shocks Seattle (NEWSPAPER ARTICLE) ~
PATRICK MCMAHON   **78**

Because I could not stop for Death (POEM) ~
EMILY DICKINSON   **91**

38 Who Saw Murder Didn't Call Police (ESSAY) ~
MARTIN GANSBERG   **99**

Growing Up Game (ESSAY) ~ BRENDA PETERSON   **104**

The Story of an Hour (SHORT STORY) ~ KATE CHOPIN   **109**

Looking Up at Something (POEM) ~ DENNIS SAMPSON   **116**

The Tell-Tale Heart (SHORT STORY) ~ EDGAR ALLAN POE   **127**

The Hammer Man (SHORT STORY) ~ TONI CADE BAMBARA   **171**

Description

Reflections   (ESSAY) ~ KENNY JACKSON   **18**

The New Testament   (NONFICTION EXCERPT) ~
JAMES MCBRIDE   **33**

Po Folks: Off with Their Heads   (SHORT STORY) ~
MARGO WILLIAMS   **42**

Along the Tortilla Curtain   (ESSAY) ~ PETE HAMILL   **50**

A Fable for Tomorrow   (NONFICTION EXCERPT) ~
RACHEL CARSON   **55**

What We Can Learn from Japan's Prisons   (ESSAY) ~
JAMES WEBB   **64**

Familiar Footing   (ESSAY) ~ CHERYL SABA   **71**

Body Ritual among the Nacirema   (ESSAY) ~ HORACE MINER   **93**

Illustration

An Indian Father's Plea: Don't Label My Son a "Slow Learner"
(LETTER) ~ ROBERT LAKE   **2**

Childless with Children   (ESSAY) ~ ANDY STEINER   **151**

In Praise of the F Word   (ESSAY) ~ MARY SHERRY   **167**

Racism and Sexism in the Media   (TEXTBOOK EXCERPT) ~
MARGARET ANDERSEN AND HOWARD F. TAYLOR   **186**

To Pet or Not to Pet?   (ESSAY) ~ NADYA LABI   **192**

Comparison/Contrast

A Fable for Tomorrow   (NONFICTION EXCERPT) ~
RACHEL CARSON   **55**

In the Suburbs   (POEM) ~ LOUIS SIMPSON   **59**

The House on Mango Street   (FICTION) ~ SANDRA CISNEROS   **61**

What We Can Learn from Japan's Prisons   (ESSAY) ~
JAMES WEBB   **64**

To Pet or Not to Pet?   (ESSAY) ~ NADYA LABI   **192**

Definition

Is There Life on Mars?   (TEXTBOOK EXCERPT) ~ TERESA AUDESIRK AND GERALD AUDESIRK   **47**

Dreaming: Mysterious Mental Activity During Sleep   (TEXTBOOK EXCERPT) ~ SAMUEL L. WOOD AND ELLEN GREEN WOOD   **81**

The Right Chemistry   (ESSAY) ~ ANASTASIA TOUFEXIS   **133**

Health Watch: Eating Disorders—Betrayal of the Body   (TEXTBOOK EXCERPT) ~ TERESA AUDESIRK AND GERALD AUDESIRK   **139**

Fear Not   (ESSAY) ~ JEFFREY KLUGER   **142**

Childless with Children   (ESSAY) ~ ANDY STEINER   **151**

What Is Poverty?   (SPEECH) ~ JO GOODWIN PARKER   **158**

A Valuable Tapestry   (RADIO BROADCAST) ~ SHIRLEY HART BERRY   **164**

Explanation

The Shakers   (TEXTBOOK EXCERPT) ~ JAMES HENRETTA, DAVID BRODY, SUSAN WARE, AND MARILYNN S. JOHNSON   **26**

Is There Life on Mars?   (TEXTBOOK EXCERPT) ~ TERESA AUDESIRK AND GERALD AUDESIRK   **47**

Dreaming: Mysterious Mental Activity During Sleep   (TEXTBOOK EXCERPT) ~ SAMUEL L. WOOD AND ELLEN GREEN WOOD   **81**

Last Flight   (LETTER) ~ ISAO MATSUO   **88**

Now Hear This: Shhhhhhhhhh   (TEXTBOOK EXCERPT) ~ JEANETTE BATZ   **119**

Hooked on Anger   (ESSAY) ~ RUSSELL BAKER   **124**

The Right Chemistry   (ESSAY) ~ ANASTASIA TOUFEXIS   **133**

Health Watch: Eating Disorders—Betrayal of the Body   (TEXTBOOK EXCERPT) ~ TERESA AUDESIRK AND GERALD AUDESIRK   **139**

The Powwow at the End of the World   (POEM) ~ SHERMAN ALEXIE   **179**

Racism and Sexism in the Media   (TEXTBOOK EXCERPT) ~ MARGARET ANDERSEN AND HOWARD F. TAYLOR   **186**

Process Analysis

Body Ritual among the Nacirema   (Essay) ~ Horace Miner   **93**

The Right Chemistry   (Essay) ~ Anastasia Toufexis   **133**

Persuasion

An Indian Father's Plea: Don't Label My Son a "Slow Learner"
(Letter) ~ Robert Lake   **2**

Growing Up Game   (Essay) ~ Brenda Peterson   **104**

Now Hear This: Shhhhhhhhhh   (Essay) ~ Jeanette Batz   **119**

Hooked on Anger   (Essay) ~ Russell Baker   **124**

In Praise of the F Word   (Essay) ~ Mary Sherry   **167**

*A Dose of Reality: The Truth about North America's Greatest
Drug Problem. Ritalin.*   (Essay) ~ Richard De Grandpre   **182**

Classification

Fear Not   (Essay) ~ Jeffrey Kluger   **142**

Dialogue

Girl   (Short Story) ~ Jamaica Kincaid   **23**

Metaphor

Mother to Son   (Poem) ~ Langston Hughes   **31**

Preface

I talk to so many students who tell me, "I hate English!" or " I'm not good at writing!" or "Reading is boring!" *The Big Picture* is my attempt to convince you that reading can be fun, that students can be good writers, and that nobody has to hate English. You already know so much about English, reading, and writing that if you wrote it all down it would fill a library. Furthermore, you have already spent a great deal of your time in school learning about the various components of written language: spelling, grammar, vocabulary, sentences, paragraphs, and much more. This text, then, is designed to help you broaden and refine your reading and writing skills; the readings and the activities will assist you in making the connections you need to bring all the pieces together and understand the big picture.

In *The Big Picture*, you will encounter forty thought-provoking readings on a number of subjects. The readings are organized around five general themes: People, Places, Events, Phenomena, and Issues. Accompanying each reading are six activities:

PREREADING

The prereading activities are designed to warm you up to the specific topic addressed in the reading. These activities will have you free writing, doing research, or engaging in collaborative activities with your peers.

ANNOTATING

Annotating is a method of underlining material in a reading and taking notes in the margins. It is a very important way to connect with reading material and to understand the reading material more fully. Each reading includes an annotating prompt that will help you focus your annotations.

EXPLORING VOCABULARY

Having a well-developed vocabulary is vital to being a good reader and a good writer. Consequently, each reading includes an activity that will help you expand your vocabulary and become familiar with using a dictionary and a thesaurus.

PROFILING

After reading you will be asked to complete a profile sheet. The profile sheets will assist you in gathering literal and implied information about the reading, which will hone your analytical and reading skills. These profile sheets may also serve as a basis for your own writing.

EXPLORING THE TEXT

You will find a set of questions after each reading that will prompt you to examine the way the text is written. When answering these questions, you will be asked to identify main ideas, identify an author's purpose, characterize an author's tone, or analyze other aspects of the text. Examining a text this way will help you become a better reader and help you become more aware of the kinds of decisions writers make.

EXPLORING IDEAS

The questions in this section will require you to examine the content of a reading and/or examine yourself in relation to the ideas in the reading. Here you might be asked to agree or disagree with an author's ideas, interpret a quote, or share a personal experience. These questions will provide you with an opportunity to develop your own ideas about a topic.

One of the keys to becoming a better reader and a better writer is exposing yourself to the written word. Consequently, at the end of each unit, you will find a list of suggestions for reading books about the theme of the unit. The books listed are fascinating and wonderful and reading them will strengthen your reading abilities. In addition, you will find a list of suggestions for summarizing essays from the unit and a list of possible writing assignments.

The Big Picture also contains several appendices with useful information for you to reference as you go through the cycle of prereading, reading and annotating, exploring vocabulary, profiling, exploring the text, and exploring ideas.

CONTEXT CLUES

Here you can access two specific strategies for defining words in the readings before consulting a dictionary.

WORD PARTS

In this appendix you will find lists of common prefixes, word roots, and suffixes that will help you define words in your reading.

SUMMARY WRITING

The third appendix outlines a strategy for summarizing essays; it includes a sample summary as well.

CHARACTERISTICS OF GOOD WRITING

Appendix Four provides a brief description of the components of good writing (controlling idea, support, unity, logical order, transition, and clarity).

THE WRITING PROCESS

The final appendix suggests a specific sequence of writing to help you achieve the characteristics of good writing.

All these components make up *The Big Picture*. While using this book, I hope you learn more about reading and writing than you thought you could, and I hope you enjoy your semester. Good luck to you.

Unit I

PEOPLE

An Indian Father's Plea:
Don't Label My Son a "Slow Learner" (LETTER)

ROBERT LAKE

PREREADING

Free write about a time you felt helpless and needed someone—a parent, a sibling, a friend, or even a stranger—to stand up for you. If you cannot think of such a time, free write about a time when you had to stand up for someone else.

ANNOTATING

While reading, underline any words, phrases, or sentences you find surprising. Write notes in the margins explaining why you are surprised.

Dear Teacher,

I would like to introduce you to my son, Wind-Wolf. He is probably what you would consider a typical Indian kid. He was born and raised on the reservation. He has black hair, dark brown eyes, and an olive complexion. And like so many Indian children his age, he is shy and quiet in the classroom. He is five years old, in kindergarten, and I can't understand why you have already labeled him a "slow learner." (1)

At the age of five, he has already been through quite an education compared with his peers in Western society. As his first introduction into this world, he was bonded to his mother and to the Mother Earth in a traditional native childbirth ceremony. And he has been continuously cared for by his mother, father, sisters, cousins, aunts, uncles, grandparents, and extended tribal family since this ceremony. (2)

From his mother's warm and loving arms, Wind-Wolf was placed in a secure and specially designed Indian baby basket. His father and the medicine elders conducted another ceremony that served to bond him with the essence of his genetic father, the Great Spirit, the Grandfather Sun, and the Grandmother Moon. This was all done to introduce him properly into the new and natural world, not the world of artificiality, and to protect his sensitive and delicate soul. It is our people's way of showing the newborn respect, ensuring that he starts his life on the path of spirituality. The traditional Indian baby basket became his turtle shell and served as the first seat for his classroom. He was strapped in for safety, protected from injury by the willow roots and hazel wood construction. The basket was made by a tribal elder who had gathered her materials with prayer and in a ceremonial way. It is the same kind of basket that our people have used for thousands of years. It is specially designed to provide the child with the kind of knowledge and experience he will need to survive in his culture and environment.   (3)

Wind-Wolf was strapped in snugly with a deliberate restriction upon his arms and legs. Although you in Western society may argue that such a method serves to hinder motor-skill development and abstract reasoning, we believe it forces the child to first develop his intuitive faculties, rational intellect, symbolic thinking, and five senses.   (4)

Wind-Wolf was with his mother constantly, closely bonded physically, as she carried him on her back or held him in front while breast-feeding. She carried him everywhere she went, and every night he slept with both parents. Because of this, Wind-Wolf's educational setting was not only a "secure" environment, but it was also very colorful, complicated, sensitive, and diverse.   (5)

He has been with his mother at the ocean at daybreak when she made her prayers and gathered fresh seaweed from the rocks. He has sat with his uncles in a rowboat on the river while they fished with gil nets, and he has watched and listened to elders as they told creation stories and animal legends and sang songs around the campfires.   (6)

He has attended the sacred and ancient White Deerskin Dance of his people and is well acquainted with the cultures and languages of other tribes. He has been with his mother when she gathered herbs for healing and watched his tribal aunts and grandmothers gather and prepare traditional foods such as acorn, smoked salmon, eel, and deer meat. He has played with abalone shells, pine nuts, iris grass string, and leather while watching the women make beaded jewelry and traditional native regalia. He has had many opportunities to watch his father, uncles, and ceremonial leaders use different kinds of colorful feathers and sing different kinds of songs while preparing for the sacred dances and rituals. (7)

As he grew older, Wind-Wolf began to crawl out of his baby basket, develop his motor skills, and explore the world around him. When frightened or sleepy, he would always return to the basket, as a turtle withdraws in his shell. Such an inward journey allows one to reflect in privacy on what he has learned and to carry new knowledge deeply into the unconscious and the soul. Shapes, sizes, colors, texture, sound, smell, feeling, taste, and the learning process are therefore functionally integrated—the physical and spiritual, matter and energy, conscious and unconscious, individual and social. (8)

This kind of learning goes beyond the basics of distinguishing the difference between rough and smooth, square and round, hard and soft, black and white, similarities and extremes. (9)

For example, Wind-Wolf was with his mother in South Dakota while she danced for seven days straight in the hot sun, fasting and piercing herself in the sacred Sun Dance Ceremony of a distant tribe. He has been doctored in a number of different healing ceremonies by medicine men and women from diverse places ranging from Alaska and Arizona to New York and California. He has been in more than 20 different sacred sweat lodge rituals—used by native tribes to purify mind, body, and soul—since he was three years old, and he has already been exposed to many different religions of his racial brothers: Protestant, Catholic, Asian Buddhist, and Tibetan Lamaist. (10)

It takes a long time to absorb and reflect on these kinds of experiences, so maybe that is why you think my Indian child is a slow learner. His aunts and grandmothers taught him to count and know his numbers while they sorted out the complex materials used to make the abstract designs in the native baskets. He listened to this mother count each and every bead and sort them out numerically according to color while she painstakingly made complex beaded belts and necklaces. He learned his basic numbers by helping his father count and sort the rocks to be used in the sweat lodge—7 rocks for a medicine sweat, say, or 13 for the summer solstice ceremony (the rocks are later heated and doused with water to create purifying steam).   (11)

And he was taught to learn mathematics by counting the sticks we use in our traditional native hand game. So I realize he may be slow in grasping the methods and tools that you are now using in your classroom, ones quite familiar to his white peers, but I hope you will be patient with him. It takes time to adjust to a new cultural system and learn new things. He is not culturally "disadvantaged," but he is culturally different. If you ask him how many months there are in a year, he will probably tell you 13. He will respond this way because he has been taught by our traditional people that there are 13 full moons in a year according to the native tribal calendar and that there are really 13 planets in our solar system and 13 tail feathers in a perfectly balanced eagle, the most powerful kind of bird to use in ceremony and healing. But he also knows that some eagles may have 12 tail feathers or 7, that they do not all have the same number. He knows that the flicker has exactly 10 tail feathers, they are red and black, representing the directions of east and west, life and death; and that this bird is considered a "fire" bird, a power used in native doctoring and healing. He can probably count more than 40 different kinds of birds, tell you and his peers what kind of bird each is and where it lives, the seasons in which it appears, and how it is used in a sacred ceremony. He may have trouble writing his name on a piece of paper, but he knows how to say it and many other things in different Indian languages. He is not fluent yet because he is only 5 years old and required by law to attend your educational system, learn your language, your values, your way of thinking, and your methods of teaching and learning.   (12)

So you see, all these influences together make him somewhat shy and quiet—and perhaps "slow" according to your standards. But Wind-Wolf was not prepared for his first tentative foray into your wo'' were you appreciative of his culture. On the first d difficulty with his name. You wanted to call him W somehow Wolf must be his middle name. The stude laughed at him, causing further embarrassment. Whi teach him your new methods, helping him learn nev discovery and adapt to his new learning environment, he may be looking out the window as if day-dreaming. Why? Because he has been taught to watch and study the changes in nature. It is hard for him to make the appropriate psychic switch from the right to the left hemisphere of the brain when he sees the leaves turning bright colors and the geese heading south, and the squirrels scurrying around for nuts to get ready for a harsh winter. In his heart, in his young mind, and almost by instinct, he knows that this is the time of year he is supposed to be with his people gathering and preparing fish, deer meat, and native plants and herbs, and learning his assigned tasks in this role. He is caught between two worlds, torn by different cultural systems.   (13)

Yesterday, for the third time in 2 weeks, he came home crying and said he wanted to have his hair cut. He said he doesn't have any friends at school because they make fun of his long hair. I tried to explain to him that in our culture, long hair is a sign of masculinity and balance and is a source of power. But he remained adamant in his position.   (14)

To make matters worse, he recently encountered his first harsh case of racism. Wind-Wolf had managed to adopt at least one good school friend. On the way home from school one day he asked his new pal if he wanted to come home and play until supper. That was OK with Wind-Wolf's mother, who was walking with them. When they all got to the little friend's house, the two boys ran inside to ask permission while Wind-Wolf's mother waited. But the other boy's mother lashed out: "It is OK if you have to play with him at school, but we don't have to allow these kind of people in our house!" When my wife asked why not, the other boy's mother answered, "Because you are Indians and we are white, and I don't want my kids growing up with your kind of people."   (15)

So now my young Indian child does not want to go to school anymore (even though we cut his hair). He feels that he does not belong. He is the only Indian child in your class, and he is well aware of the fact. Instead of being proud of his race, heritage, and culture, he feels ashamed. When he watches television, he asks why white people hate us so much and why they take everything away from us. He asks why other kids in school are not taught about the power, beauty, and ce of nature or provided with an opportunity to experience the round them first hand. He says he hates living in the city and that he misses his Indian cousins and friends. He asks why one white girl at school who is a friend always tells him "I like you Wind-Wolf, because you are a good Indian."   (16)

Now he refuses to sing his native songs, play with his Indian artifacts, learn his language, or participate in his sacred ceremonies. When I ask him to go to an urban powwow or help me with a sacred sweat lodge ritual, he says no because that is "weird" and he doesn't want his friends in school to think that he doesn't believe in God.   (17)

So dear teacher, I want to introduce you to my son, Wind-Wolf, who is not really a "typical" kid after all. He stems from a long line of hereditary chiefs, medicine men and women, and ceremonial leaders whose accomplishments and unique forms of knowledge are still studied and recorded in contemporary books. He has seven different tribal systems flowing through his veins; he is even part white. I want my child to succeed in school and in life. I don't want him to be a drop-out or juvenile delinquent or to end up on drugs or alcohol because he is made to feel inferior or because of discrimination. I want him to be proud of his rich heritage and culture, and I would like him to develop the necessary abilities to adapt to and succeed in both cultures. But I need your help.   (18)

What you say and what you do in the classroom, what you teach and how you teach it, and what you say and what you don't will have a significant effect on the potential failure or success of my child. Please remember that this is the primary year of his education and development. All I ask is that you work with me, not against me, to help educate my child in the best way.   (19)

My son Wind-Wolf is not an empty glass coming into your class to be filled. He is a full basket coming into a different environment and society with something special to share. Please let him share his knowledge, heritage, and culture with you and his peers.   (20)

EXPLORING VOCABULARY

Define the following terms: *ethnicity, culture, values, heritage, custom, tradition, minority, prejudice,* and *discrimination.* In a small group or with the class, discuss how these concepts relate to the reading.

PROFILING PEOPLE

Using the profile sheet on page 40, write a profile of Wind-Wolf. You may have to read between the lines—or make inferences—to address some of the categories. When you are finished, discuss your answers with a small group of your peers or with the entire class.

EXPLORING THE TEXT

1. What is the main idea of this letter? Is it implicit or explicit?
2. Why did Lake write this letter?
3. To whom is Lake really writing this letter?
4. Why did Lake choose to write a letter instead of an essay, a short story, or a poem?

EXPLORING IDEAS

1. Are you surprised by Wind-Wolf's experiences in school or out of school? (Review your annotations.)
2. If you were Wind-Wolf's teacher, could you defend your behavior? How?
3. What responsibility, if any, does Wind-Wolf's father have for the difficulty Wind-Wolf is experiencing?
4. What advice can you give Wind-Wolf to help him adjust to his new environment?

The Good Daughter (Essay)

CAROLINE HWANG

PREREADING

Free write about what your parents expect you to do with your adult life. You may want to consider their expectations about your education, career, and marriage.

ANNOTATING

While reading, underline any words that you cannot readily define. In the margins, write a possible definition for each word.

The moment I walked into the dry-cleaning store, I knew the woman behind the counter was from Korea, like my parents. To show her that we shared a heritage, and possibly get a fellow countrymen's discount, I tilted my head forward, in shy imitation of a traditional bow.   (1)

"Name?" she asked, not noticing my attempted obeisance.   (2)

"Hwang," I answered.   (3)

"Hwang? Are you Chinese?"   (4)

Her question caught me off-guard. I was used to hearing such queries from non-Asians who think Asians all look alike, but never from one of my own people. Of course, the only Koreans I knew were my parents and their friends, people who've never asked me where I came from, since they knew better than I.   (5)

I ransacked my mind for the Korean words that would tell her who I was. It's always struck me as funny (in a mirthless sort of way) that I can more readily say "I am Korean" in Spanish, German and even Latin than I can in the language of my ancestry. In the end, I told her in English.   (6)

The dry-cleaning woman squinted as though trying to see past the glare of my strangeness, repeating my surname under her breath. "Oh, *Fxuang*," she said, doubling over with laughter. "You don't know how to speak your name." (7)

I flinched. Perhaps I was particularly sensitive at the time, having just dropped out of graduate school. I had torn up my map for the future, the one that said not where I was going but who I was. My sense of identity was already disintegrating. (8)

When I got home, I called my parents to ask why they had never bothered to correct me. "Big deal," my mother said, sounding more flippant than I knew she intended. (Like many people who learn English in a classroom, she uses idioms that don't always fit the occasion.) "So what if you can't pronounce your name? You are American," she said. (9)

Though I didn't challenge her explanation, it left me unsatisfied. The fact is, my cultural identity is hardly that clear-cut. (10)

My parents immigrated to this country 30 years ago, two years before I was born. They told me often, while I was growing up, that, if I wanted to, I could be president someday, that here my grasp would be as long as my reach. (11)

To ensure that I reaped all the advantages of this country, my parents saw to it that I became fully assimilated. So, like any American of my generation, I whiled away my youth strolling malls and talking on the phone, rhapsodizing over Andrew McCarthy's blue eyes or analyzing the meaning of a certain upperclassman's offer of a ride to the Homecoming football game. (12)

To my parents, I am all American, and the sacrifices they made in leaving Korea—including my mispronounced name—pale in comparison to the opportunities those sacrifices gave me. They do not see that I straddle two cultures, nor that I feel displaced in the only country I know. I identify with Americans, but Americans do not identify with me. I've never known what it's like to belong to a community—neither one at large, nor of an extended family. I know more about Europe than the continent my ancestors unmistakably come from. I sometimes wonder, as I did that day in the dry cleaner's, if I would be a happier person had my parents stayed in Korea. (13)

I first began to consider this thought around the time I decided to go to graduate school. It had been a compromise: My parents wanted me to go to law school; I wanted to skip the starch-collar track and be a writer—the hungrier the better. But after 20-some years of following their wishes and meeting their expectations, I couldn't bring myself to disobey or disappoint. A writing career is riskier than law, I remember thinking. If I'm a failure and my life is a washout, then what does that make my parents' lives? (14)

I know that many of my friends had to choose between pleasing their parents and being true to themselves. But for the children of immigrants, the choice seems more complicated, a happy outcome impossible. By making the biggest move of their lives for me, my parents indentured me to the largest imaginable debt—I owe them the fulfillment of their hopes for me. (15)

It tore me up inside to suppress my dream, but I went to school for a Ph.D. in English literature, thinking I had found the perfect compromise. I would be able to write at least about books while pursuing a graduate degree. Predictably, it didn't work out. How could I labor for five years in a program I had no passion for? When I finally left school, my parents were disappointed, but since it wasn't what they wanted me to do, they weren't devastated. I, on the other hand, felt I was staring at the bottom of the abyss. I had seen the flaw in my life of halfwayness, in my planned life of compromises. (16)

I hadn't thought about my love life, but I had a vague plan to make concessions there, too. Though they raised me as an American, my parents expect me to marry someone Korean and give them grandchildren who look like them. This didn't seem like such a huge request when I was 14, but now I don't know what I'm going to do. I've never been in love with someone I dated, or dated someone I loved. Since I can't bring myself even to entertain the thought of marrying the non-Korean men I'm attracted to, I've been dating only those I know I can stay clear-headed about.) And as I near that age when the question of marriage stalks every relationship, I can't help but wonder if my parents' expectations are responsible for the lack of passion in my life. (17)

My parents didn't want their daughter to be Korean, but they don't want her fully American either. Children of immigrants are living paradoxes. We are the first generation and the last. We are in this country for its opportunities, yet filial duty binds us. When my parents boarded the plane, they knew they were embarking on a rough trip. I don't think they imagined the rocks in the path of their daughter who can't even pronounce her own name.   (18)

EXPLORING VOCABULARY

Share the words you've underlined while reading with a small group of your classmates. (Review your annotations.) As a group, try to figure out the meaning of the words by using context clues and/or word parts. Then check your definitions with the dictionary.

PROFILING PEOPLE

Using the profile sheet on page 40, write a profile of Hwang. You may have to read between the lines—or make inferences—to answer some of the questions. When you are finished, discuss your answers with a small group of your peers or with the entire class.

EXPLORING THE TEXT

1. What is the main idea? Is it implicit or explicit?
2. What is the author's purpose?
3. Why does the author open with a scenario? Is the scenario effective?

EXPLORING IDEAS

1. What do Hwang's parents expect of her?
2. How would Hwang's parents feel if they read this essay?
3. Is Hwang's experience particular to children of immigrants or do people whose families have been in America for generations have similar experiences?
4. How do your parents' expectations of you compare with Hwang's parents' expectations?
5. In paragraph 10, Hwang writes, "The fact is, my cultural identity is hardly that clear-cut." What does she mean? Is your cultural identity clear-cut?

Dead Man Walking (Book Excerpt)

Sister Helen Prejean

PREREADING

Free write for ten minutes about a time you befriended someone that no one else liked—or write about a time when you could have befriended someone that no one else liked but did not. Why didn't you?

ANNOTATING

While reading, underline any words, phrases, or sentences that tell you how Sister Prejean feels about Patrick Sonnier. In the margins, briefly describe her feelings.

The red block letters say "Death Row." (1)

My stomach can read the letters better than my brain. (2)

I pace slowly back and forth in the room and keep trying to take deep breaths, to settle down. I am allowed two hours for my visit. That seems like a very long time. I'm doubly tense. One, I am locked behind four—I count them—doors in this strange, unreal place. Two, I am about to meet and talk to someone who killed two people. Letters are one thing, but just two of us like this talking for two hours? (3)

I hear him before I see him. I can hear the rattle of chains on his legs scraping across the floor and I can hear his voice. He is laughing and teasing the guard. I detect a Cajun accent. (4)

"Hi, Pat, I made it," I say. (5)

"Am I glad to see *you*, Sister," he says. (6)

He is freshly shaven and his black hair is combed into a wave in front. A handsome face, open, smiling. Not the face I had seen in the photo. He has on a clean blue denim shirt and jeans. His hands are cuffed to a wide brown leather belt at his waist. He has brought me a gift: a picture frame made out of intricately folded cigarette packages. "I made it for you," he says, and he explains that the biggest challenge had been collecting enough of the wrappers from the others on the tier. He is bright and talkative and tells me of some recent letters from college students whom I have referred to him. (7)

"I was always a loner growing up. I've never had so many friends," he says, and he tells in detail what each pen pal has said and how he has responded. He keeps a checklist: "letters received—letters answered" and the date next to each. (8)

He smokes one cigarette after another and he has to lean his head far down to reach the cigarette because his hands are cuffed to the belt. He is obviously very happy to have someone to talk to. Contact with someone in the outside world goes a very long way in this place, where, I soon learn, mail is rare and visits rarer. (9)

As we talk I find myself looking at his hands—clean, shapely hands, moving expressively despite the handcuffs as he talks. These hands that made the nice picture frame for me also held a rifle that killed. The fingernails are bitten down to the quick. (10)

He tells me again of receiving the first letter from me and how the name Helen had made him think at first it was from his ex-"old lady," and he wanted to have nothing to do with her because she was the one who had told the sheriff where to find him, warning that he was dangerous and heavily armed, and the scowl is there and he stares past me as he talks. He can't believe his good fortune, he says, that I have come into his life out of the blue like this, and he thanks me profusely for making the long drive to come and see him. (11)

The way he was teasing the guard and the way he thanks me and is talking to me now—I can tell he likes to please people. (12)

He hasn't done well with women, he admits—lived with several but always "busted up." He has a little girl, Star, eleven years old, but she is with foster parents and her mother is in Texas and he says that his child was born when he was serving time in Angola for stealing a truck, and the first time he laid eyes on her was the day he got out of prison because he went right to where his "first old lady" was living and there was the child, playing in the front yard, and he had swooped her into his arms and said, "I'm your daddy," and her mother had appeared at the front door with a shot gun because she thought someone was trying to kidnap the child and he had called out to her, "It's me. I'm back. I want to see my kid." But the first thing he had done when he stepped out of the gates at Angola was to get a case of beer, and by the time the Greyhound bus had pulled into St. Martinville he was pretty "tanked" and he and the woman had "gotten into it" that night and he smashed up some furniture and she threw him out and he had gone to his mother's.   (13)

He never has been one to share his feelings, he says, because when he was a kid growing up his mother and father used to fight a lot and they separated when he was six and his sister was three and Eddie was just a baby. His mother went on welfare because his daddy never did come through with child support and the welfare check would run out and they'd be hungry and he and Eddie would hunt deer and rabbit. He chuckles remembering how his mother would help them with the rabbit hunt and it was always her job to put the dead rabbits in a sack and to "finish them off" with a stick if they weren't dead yet. "And we'd be stalking along and behind us we'd hear *whack, whack, whack*—Mama beating the hell out of those rabbits."   (14)

I cringe, but he tells the incident nonchalantly. I am thinking of the clobbered rabbits. He is thinking of the food.   (15)

Once, he says, he and Eddie couldn't find a deer so they shot a neighbor's cow and skinned it and brought it home. "Mama knew this was no more a deer than the man in the moon, but she didn't say nothing 'cause we were all so hungry. She fixed us a good roast that night and you could smell it cooking all through the house."   (16)

They often hunted at night. "Isn't it against the law to hunt at night?" I ask. "Yeah," he says," but we didn't worry about that."   (17)

As kids they moved from mother to father and back again, he says, and by the time he was fourteen he had changed schools seven or eight times. He got only as far as eighth grade, dropped out when he was fifteen, forged his mother's signature on an application form, and went to work as a roustabout on the oil rigs. Later, he got his license and drove eighteen-wheelers and he had liked that best. From the age of nine, he says, he was on probation with juvenile authorities for burglaries, disturbing the peace, trespassing. "Mama couldn't do anything with me and she'd have Daddy come get me out of trouble."   (18)

His daddy was a sharecropper and one of the best things he got from him, he says, is his love of work. At the age of seven he picked cotton, potatoes, and peppers alongside his father, and as he got older,

when it was harvesting time for the sugar cane, "there I'd be walking
to school and see those open fields and I'd drop my books on the side
of the road and head out into the fields." He hopes that maybe
someday he can "hand back the chair" and work in the fields here,
driving one of the tractors.   (19)

He stands up and I try to adjust my view of him because it is hard
to see through the heavy mesh screen and he tells me to look down
sometimes. "This screen can really do a number on your eyes."   (20)

He talks and talks and talks, and I am easing up inside because I was
wondering how much I'd have to keep the conversation going, and
now I can see that all I have to do is listen.   (21)

"Daddy took me to a bar when I was twelve and told me to pick
my whiskey and there were all these bottles behind the bar and I
pointed and said I'd take the one with the pretty turkey on it and the
guys in the bar laughed and Daddy laughed too." He laughs. "We got
drunk as a couple of coots and there we were at one in the morning
trying to make it home on our bicycles, weaving and hitting every
garbage can along the road."   (22)

He has feelings for his father, I can tell by the way he speaks of him, and
he says that when he and his cousin, Robert, had been arrested for stealing
a truck (the plan was to run away to Texas and start a new life) Robert's
father had come to the jail to talk to the authorities and had gotten his boy
off, but by then his own father was dead—cancer of the liver—and so Pat
served time in Angola. "But you can bet your bottom dollar that if Daddy
had been living, he'd been there to get me out," he says.   (23)

The guard announces that visiting time is over.   (24)

I rise to leave. I thank him for the picture frame and promise to
come back in a month, and again he thanks me for making the long
drive. "Be careful on that highway," he says. "People drive crazy." (25)

I have a roaring headache when I emerge from the prison, and I
take two Bufferins before I begin the drive back. Pure tension. I have
never been in such a strange place in my life. When I get home, I
promise myself, I'm going to take a bath to wash the place off me.   (26)

EXPLORING VOCABULARY

With a small group of your classmates, come up with a list of five or six
adjectives to describe Sonnier's childhood. Be sure you can support your

choices by pointing to specific passages in the text. Share your list with the class.

PROFILING PEOPLE

Using the profile sheet on page 40, write a profile of Patrick Sonnier. You may have to read between the lines—or make inferences—to answer some of the questions. When you are finished, discuss your answers with a small group of your peers or with the entire class.

EXPLORING THE TEXT

1. What do you learn about Prejean from reading this excerpt?
2. From what point of view does Prejean write this excerpt? Why does she choose this point of view?
3. Why does Prejean give us so many details about Sonnier's appearance?
4. Look at the passages in which Prejean uses dialogue and those in which she tells us what Sonnier said. Which passages are more effective? Why?

EXPLORING IDEAS

1. Do you support capital punishment? Why or why not?
2. How does Prejean feel about Sonnier? Do her feelings change? (Review your annotations.)
3. Describe Sonnier's relationship with his mother, his father, and his brother? Do these relationships in any way explain his behavior?
4. Could you visit and befriend someone on death row? Why or why not?

Reflections (Essay)

Kenny Jackson

PREREADING

Look up the word *chemotherapy* in a dictionary and in an encyclopedia. Find out what it is, how it works, and what effects it has on the human body. Share your research with the class.

ANNOTATING

While reading, underline the words, phrases, and sentences that express how Jackson feels as he goes through his day.

"When I count to three, you will feel a stick." (1)

I shut my eyes and pray, "Oh, God, please don't let this hurt." I think about cool ocean water and how it feels when you dive into a wave. (2)

When I open my eyes, I am at home in bed. I look at the alarm clock. It's 5:45 a.m. My biological clock has awakened me early today. It's Monday, a cool autumn morning, and my bed feels so warm and comfortable. It's barely light when I pull back the wooden blinds, but I can see that the grass is glistening with a heavy dew and that the cows are in the field. In the distance, I can hear a rooster. (3)

This Monday will be like the past twenty-six Mondays: vein punctures, blood counts, Doctor Peterson, and chemotherapy. (4)

The alarm clock goes off at 6:00 a.m. I get out of bed, and my mom and I leave the house by 6:30. The drive to the chemo clinic at the University of North Carolina hospital takes about forty-five minutes. Mom is driving; I look out the window at the quiet country, which is so beautiful this time of year. I take this time to mentally prepare and pray for intercessions from the Holy Father. (5)

The car is warm, and I feel a bit drowsy. I sit back, relax, and close my eyes. I can see Barbara standing next to me, patting my shoulder, and telling me to breathe. Her smile always makes me feel secure, and her loving manner brings a sense of calm to all the patients in the cancer center. Barbara smiles a lot and smells of soft summer flowers; her hair is nicely styled.   (6)

When she is caring for me—taking my blood—I like to look outside the big window in the triage unit at my favorite tree. I heard that some of the trees on the UNC campus are 500 years old. I like to ponder the history of the trees—what they have seen and how many people have enjoyed their beauty. I imagine that many people don't even notice their beauty because they are too busy living their lives. Cancer, however, will slow your life down and make you take notice. I used to think I was so strong that I could probably destroy one of those trees if I wanted to. Now, I think differently.   (7)

As we get closer to the hospital, I wonder what has happened to my life. Why do I have to face cancer? I am in remission now, but I have had six months worth of chemotherapy in the last four months. During those four months, I have learned to give myself shots, my body has been inundated with drugs, and I have lost every hair I had. Today, though, all that is over. Today I am one of the happiest people in the world because today is my last chemotherapy treatment. This whole journey started on June 24, 1996, with an upper endoscopy, and will end today, November 4, 1996. It's almost Thanksgiving, and I truly have a lot to be thankful for this year. I went into remission pretty early in my treatment, so I am hoping that the cancer is long gone.   (8)

Mom and I walk into the chemotherapy ward at about 7:45. The waiting room is upbeat; everyone is laughing and watching *The Today Show*. You can recognize the veteran patients because we are less uptight; we have seen each other before and there is a strong camaraderie between us. The new patients have blank faces and far-off looks in their eyes. Basically they look like their lives have been destroyed, and they are holding on for dear life. They will learn that somehow life goes on, but not life like they've ever known it before. Life will be much richer and more meaningful to these new patients. I know that somehow, through Christ and family and friends, they will pull themselves together and move on.   (9)

I have met so many people in this waiting room. Some are still alive and doing fine now, some are still battling cancer, and some exist on another plane. Today, I am looking for Edmond; he is a Frenchman, about sixty-five years of age. He speaks with a French accent, and his wife is so in love with him. She is always right there with him, asking questions, worrying about Edmond, and looking for certainty that everything will be all right. He has a cancerous growth next to his heart. It is inoperable, so the doctors are trying to shrink it with chemo. There is something about him that I love. He's charming like one of those Frenchmen you see in the movies with a beret. He's also selfless and calm, and he has had a full life. *He's not afraid.* This morning he is talking about getting together with me and sharing a bottle of wine at one of those outside cafes in Chapel Hill. (10)

"Ken Jackson!" A nurse calls my name. I enter the chemotherapy ward, which is a bit cold and sterile. The walls are baby blue, and doctors and nurses are busy scurrying around. My first stop is triage. This is where Barbara takes my temperature, my blood pressure, and a blood sample. I sit in the famous "blood chair," she ties a rubber tourniquet around my arm, and she starts beating on it to get one of my veins to show itself. By now the chemo has taken its toll on my veins, so I sit there hoping one will appear. The veins in my wrist are irritated and protrude at least a half an inch above the skin. Finally, one appears, and Barbara begins moving the needle around in my arm trying to hit a vein. She is a pro, and she finds one. I hold my breath and watch the precious, thick red gold fill the tube. (11)

"All done," she says as she labels the tube. "You're in room five today, Dr. Peterson's room." (12)

I have known Barbara for twenty-six weeks, and as I walk away from her, I hope that she remembers me. (13)

I meet with Dr. Peterson in room five. He is a young man, around 43 years old, tall, rugged, handsome, preppy. (14)

"How do you feel today?" he asks me. (15)

"I'm fine," I say. "Ready for my last chemotherapy, but . . . but I don't know how I will ever trust my body again." (16)

"Take each day slowly. You know the symptoms, Ken, and if you have questions or need to see me, I will be here. I'm not far away." (17)

I think of Doctor Peterson as more than just my doctor; he is my friend. He has told me about his family and his life, and it seems that he's in medicine for more than just financial rewards. He really cares about his patients.   (18)

He does the usual inspection of my body: he checks the lymph nodes under my arms and in my groin area. He listens to my stomach, heart, and lungs, and he reads over my lab work. If my white blood cell count is 1500–2000, they will administer the chemo. If not, I will have to wait until next Monday. Last August, my white blood cell count was only 300, and I thought I was dying. Chemotherapy is a double-edged sword because it kills the cancer, but it also kills cells that your body needs to survive. This is why cancer patients aren't very active. Today, though, my white blood cell counts are fine. Let the chemo begin!   (19)

Dr. Peterson and I walk to the chemo ward. Rosie O'Donnell is on the television—she has been such a good friend to the UNC cancer patients. My mom is waiting for me. I get into a bed and Lisa, my nurse, comes and asks me if I want anything to eat or drink. She's very compassionate and sweet, but I don't want anything. Today, I will receive five different chemotherapy drugs; they will be in a liquid intravenous drip. Lisa and another nurse have a bit of trouble finding my vein, so they call in Tom, the head nurse.   (20)

"So, I hear this is your last chemo," he says. He is smiling.   (21)

"Yeah, it is, if we can get my veins to cooperate."   (22)

"I have to put the tourniquet back on your arm."   (23)

I begin to cry—just a little. "Please find a vein. I don't want to have to do this next Monday." Tom wipes a tear from my cheek with his thumb. Then he got a vein on the first try—a vein just three inches above the elbow.   (24)

"Thanks." I tell him. "You were here for the first round of chemo; it seems only right that you are here for the last."   (25)

Tom smiles. "I want you to have a happy and healthy life," he says.   (26)

I close my eyes and think about cool ocean water. I always think about water because the chemo is so cold when it first goes through your veins. I wonder if I will ever be able to get back to normal, if I will ever be able to trust my body again, and if I will have a long life. I read in a book once that whenever something causes you great pain, you have to look to a higher power, pull out your inner strength, and just move forward. I have been trying to do that, and I will continue to try.   (27)

On the way out of the chemo ward, I stop in triage and look at my favorite tree. For a tree, autumn brings the lowering of the sap, which causes a dormant period. I like to think of chemo as a lowering of my body's defenses in order to bring about a stronger, healthier Ken. I can't wait to jog again, to work out, and to get back to work and to life. Like my tree, I have a chance at another spring, which means another opportunity to live an examined life. This whole experience has taught me the mystery of life: you have to live each day as if it is your last.   (28)

EXPLORING VOCABULARY

Skim over the essay again and underline the medical terms. Then find the definitions in a dictionary. Share your answers with the class.

PROFILING EVENTS

Using the profile sheet on page 40, write a profile of Jackson's last day of chemotherapy. You may have to read between the lines—or make inferences—to address some of the categories. When you are finished, discuss your answers with a small group of your peers or with the entire class.

EXPLORING THE TEXT

1. Jackson uses quite a bit of description in this essay. Which descriptions do you like the most? Why?
2. What is the time sequence in the essay? Is it easy to follow?
3. Jackson uses dialogue at several points in the essay. Is it effective? Are there any other places that dialogue would also work?
4. What is Jackson's tone?

EXPLORING IDEAS

1. Jackson seems to experience a range of emotions; what specific emotions does he feel? (Review your annotations.)
2. Two times, Jackson shares his reticence to trust his body again. Why does he feel this way?
3. Do you trust your body? Has there ever been a time when you didn't trust your body?
4. What does Jackson mean in paragraph twenty-eight by the phrase "examined life"?

Girl (SHORT STORY)

JAMAICA KINCAID

PREREADING

With a small group of your peers, brainstorm a list of behaviors or rules that your parents attempted to instill in you and your siblings. Then review the list and try to determine if any of them are gender specific—whether some of them are meant for just boys and some are meant for just girls.

ANNOTATING

While reading, underline any rules or behaviors that sound familiar to you. In the margins, note who introduced you to these rules (parent, grandparent, teacher, etc.).

Wash the white clothes on Monday and put them on the stone heap; wash the color clothes on Tuesday and put them on the clothesline to dry; don't walk barehead in the hot sun; cook pumpkin fritters in very hot sweet oil; soak your little clothes right after you take them off; when buying cotton to make yourself a nice blouse, be sure that it doesn't have gum on it, because that way it won't hold up well after a wash; soak salt fish overnight before you cook it; is it true that you sing benna in Sunday school?; always eat your food in such a way that it won't turn someone else's stomach; on Sundays try to walk like a lady and not like the slut you are so bent on becoming; don't sing benna in Sunday school; you mustn't speak to wharf-rat boys, not even to give directions; don't eat fruits on the street—flies will follow you; *but I don't sing benna on Sundays at all and never in Sunday school*; this is how to sew on a button; this is how to make a buttonhole for the button you have just sewed on; this is how to hem a dress when you see the hem coming down and so to prevent yourself from looking like the slut I know you are so bent on becoming; this is how you iron your father's khaki shirt so that is doesn't have a crease; this is how you iron your father's khaki pants so that they don't have a crease; this is how you grow okra—far from the house, because okra tree harbors red ants; when you are growing dasheen, make sure it gets plenty of water or else it makes your throat itch when you are eating it; this is how you sweep a corner; this is how you sweep a whole house; this is how you sweep a yard; this is how you smile to someone you don't like at all; this is how you smile to someone you like completely; this is how you set a table for tea; this is how you set a table for dinner; this is how you set a table for dinner with an important guest; this is how you set a table for lunch; this is how you set a table for breakfast; this is how to behave in the presence of men who don't know you very well, and this way they won't recognize immediately the slut I have warned you against becoming; be sure to wash every day, even if it is with your own spit; don't squat down to play marbles—you are not a boy, you know; don't pick people's flowers—you might catch something; don't throw stones at blackbirds, because it might not be a blackbird at all; this is how to make bread pudding; this is how to make doukona; this is how to make pepper pot; this is how to make a good medicine for a cold; this is how to make a good medicine to throw away a child before it even becomes a child; this is how to catch fish; this is how to throw back a fish you don't like, and that way something bad won't fall on you; this is how to bully a man; this is how a man bullies you; this is how to love a man, and if this doesn't work there are other ways and if they don't work don't feel too bad about giving up; this is how to spit in the air if you feel like it, and this is how to move quick so that it doesn't fall on you; this is how to make ends meet; always squeeze bread to make sure it's fresh; *but what if the baker won't let me feel the bread?*; you mean to say that after all you are really going to be the kind of woman who the baker won't let near the bread?

(1)

EXPLORING VOCABULARY

Choose five words from the reading, define the words, and find as many synonyms and antonyms for each word as possible. The thesaurus can help you with this activity, but remember that each synonym listed in the thesaurus has a subtly different meaning, so choose only those that will fit into the sentence without changing the meaning of the sentence.

PROFILING PEOPLE

Using the profile sheet on page 40, write a profile of the girl. You may have to read between the lines—or make inferences—to answer some of the questions. When you are finished, discuss your answers with a small group of your peers or with the entire class.

EXPLORING THE TEXT

1. Who is the main speaker in this story?
2. Who else is speaking? How do you know?
3. What is the main idea or theme of this story?

EXPLORING IDEAS

1. Why does Kincaid title this story "Girl"?
2. Do you think the mother's treatment of the girl is fair? Why or why not?
3. How might the mother's instructions be different if she were talking to her son instead of her daughter?
4. Compare and contrast the instructions this mother gives her daughter with the instructions your parents gave you. (Review your annotations.)

The Shakers (Textbook Excerpt)

Ｊａｍｅｓ Ｈｅｎｒｅｔｔａ, Ｄａｖｉｄ Ｂｒｏｄｙ, Ｓｕｓａｎ Ｗａｒｅ, ＡＮＤ Ｍａｒｉｌｙｎｎ Ｓ. Ｊｏｈｎｓｏｎ

PREREADING

Make a list of all the groups to which you belong (i.e., family, religious group, civic group, etc.), and then choose one entry from your list and describe the beliefs that give the group its unique identity.

ANNOTATING

While reading each of the following works, underline any information that might be used on a test if you were reading these passages for a history class. In the margins, note why.

The Shakers, the first successful American communal movement, dated back to the era of the Revolution. In 1770 Ann Lee Stanley (Mother Ann), an illiterate cook and factory worker in Manchester, England, had a vision in which God revealed to her that Adam and Eve had been banished from the Garden of Eden because of their sexual lust. Consequently, Ann Lee embraced the practice of celibacy, because it restored the purity of Paradise. In 1774 she led a band of eight followers to America, where they established a church near Albany, New York. Because of the ecstatic dances that became part of their worship, the sect became known as "Shaking Quakers" or, more simply, "Shakers . . . ." After Mother Ann's death the Shakers venerated her as the Second Coming of Christ, and they decided to withdraw from the evils of the world into strictly run communities of believers. Members had to declare themselves "sick of sin" and follow a program of confession. To the Shakers, sin was wholly the product of a society that put obstacles in the way of a chaste and self-denying life.   (1)

Shaker communities embraced the common ownership of property and vowed to abstain from politics and war. Over time Shaker doctrine also included a ban on tobacco and alcoholic drink. Most striking, Shakers eliminated marriage and made a commitment to celibacy, in accordance with Mother Ann's testimony against "the lustful gratifications of the flesh as the source and foundation of human corruption." Men and women lived apart in gender-segregated dormitories.   (2)

The Shakers believed that God was "a dual person, male and female," and that Mother Ann represented God's female element. These doctrines provided the underpinning for their attempt to banish distinctions between the sexes. In practice, Shakers maintained the traditional division of labor between men and women, but they vested the authority of governing each community—in both its religious and its economic spheres—in women and men alike, the Eldresses and Elders. And they welcomed blacks as well as whites; to Rebecca Cox Jackson, an African American seamstress from Philadelphia who joined their community, the Shakers seemed to be "loving to live forever."   (3)

Between the 1780s and 1840s Shakers founded twenty communities, mostly in New England, New York, and Ohio. . . . Their agriculture and crafts, especially furniture making, acquired a reputation for quality that enabled most of these communities to become self-sustaining and even comfortable. Thanks to this economic success and their ideology of sexual equality, Shaker communities attracted more than 3,000 converts during the 1830s, with women outnumbering men more than two to one. Because Shakers had no children of their own, they had to rely on converts and the adoption of young orphans to replenish their numbers. As these sources dried up in the 1840s and 1850s, the communities stopped growing and eventually began to decline.   (4)

Because of their celibacy, Shaker communities could never provide a model for society as a whole; at best, they could serve as a place for refuge for those fleeing life in an individualistic, industrial world. By the end of the nineteenth century most Shaker communities had disappeared, leaving as their material legacy a distinctive and much imitated furniture style.   (5)

The Mystical World of the Shakers (TEXTBOOK EXCERPT)

JAMES HENRETTA, DAVID BRODY, SUSAN WARE, AND MARILYNN S. JOHNSON

Foreigners were both attracted to and distressed by the strange religious practices they found in the United States. In either case, they made certain to include reports of revivals and communal settlements in their letters and journals. In a book recounting his travels in America in the 1830s, an anonymous British visitor describes a Shaker dance and the sect's intimate contact with spiritual worlds inaccessible to those without faith. (1)

At half past seven p.m. on the dancing days, all the members retired to their separate rooms, where they sat in solemn silence, just gazing at the stove, until their silver tones of the small tea-bell gave the signal for them to assemble in the large hall. Thither they proceeded in perfect order and solemn silence. Each had on dancing shoes; and on entering the door of the hall they walked on tip-toe, and took up their positions as follows: the brothers formed a rank on the right, and the sisters on the left, facing each other, about five feet apart. After all were in their proper places the chief Elder . . . gave an exhortation for about five minutes, concluding . . . "go forth, old men, young men and maidens and worship God with all [your] might in the dance." . . . (2)

They commenced dancing, and continued it until they were pretty well tired. During the dance the sisters kept on one side, and the brothers on the other, and not a word was spoken by any one of them. . . . [Then] each one took his or her place in an oblong circle formed around the room, and all waited to see if anyone had received a "gift," that is, an inspiration to do something odd. Then two of the sisters

would commence whirling round like a top with their eyes shut; and
continued this motion for about fifteen minutes. . . .   (3)

On some occasions when a sister had stopped whirling, she would
say, "I have a communication to make"; . . . . The first message I heard
was as follows. "Mother Ann has sent two angels to inform us that a
tribe of Indians has been round here two days, and want the brothers
and sisters to take them in." . . . The first Elder exhorted the brothers
"to take in the poor spirits and assist them to get salvation." He
afterward repeated more of what the angels had said, viz., "that Indians
were a savage tribe who had all died before Columbus discovered
America, and had been wandering about ever since.". . . Whereupon
eight or nine sisters became possessed of the spirits of Indian squaws,
and about six of the brethren became Indians. Then ensued a regular
pow-wow, with whooping and yelling and strange antics, such as
would require a Dickens to describe. . . .   (4)

At one of the meetings . . . two or three sisters commenced whirling
. . . and revealed to us that Mother Ann was present at the meeting,
and that she had brought a dozen baskets of spiritual fruit for her
children. . . . Accordingly they all stepped forth and went through the
various motions of taking fruit and eating it. You will wonder if I
helped myself to the fruit, like the rest. No; I had not faith enough to
see the baskets or the fruit. . . .   (5)

EXPLORING VOCABULARY

Read the second passage again and write down every word the narrator
uses that seems to express a negative judgment about the Shakers. Then using a thesaurus or a dictionary, find words that the author could have used
if he had wanted to express a more positive judgment about the Shakers.

PROFILING PEOPLE

Using the profile sheet on page 40, write a profile of the Shakers. You
may have to read between the lines—or make inferences—to address
some of the categories. When you are finished, discuss your answers with
a small group of your peers or with the entire class.

EXPLORING THE TEXT

1. What is the purpose of each passage?
2. Who is the intended audience of each passage?
3. Which account is more appealing to you? Why?
4. Which account is more challenging to read? Why?
5. How do these two accounts differ from one another? How do they resemble one another?

EXPLORING IDEAS

1. How were the Shakers received by society at large? How do you think they would be received today?
2. The Shakers practiced gender equality to a degree unusual for the time period. Describe the relationship between the genders.
3. In paragraph three of the first passage, the author writes: "And they welcomed blacks as well as whites. . . ." Why does the author make this point?
4. What is the predominant impression of the Shakers given by each author? Which one is more reliable? Why?
5. What information from each of these passages might be used on a history test? (Review your annotations.)

Mother to Son (POEM)

LANGSTON HUGHES

PREREADING

Find the meaning of the word *metaphor* and write out the definition.

ANNOTATING

In this poem, Langston Hughes uses a metaphor in the second line and refers back to it throughout the whole poem. While reading, underline any words or phrases that represent the metaphor he uses.

Well, son, I'll tell you:
Life for me ain't been no crystal stair.
It's had tacks in it, and splinters
And boards torn up,
And places with no carpet on the floor—   (5)
Bare.
But all the time
I'se been a-climbin' on,
And reachin' landin's,
And turnin' corners,   (10)
And sometimes goin' in the dark
Where there ain't been no light.
So, boy, don't you turn back.
Don't you set down on the steps
'Cause you finds it's kinder hard.   (15)
Don't you fall now—
For I'se still goin', honey,
I'se still climbin',
And life for me ain't been no crystal stair.

EXPLORING VOCABULARY

This poem uses informal language. What do "I'se," "kinder," and "ain't" mean?

PROFILING PEOPLE

Using the profile sheet on page 40, write a profile of the mother. You may have to read between the lines—or make inferences—to answer some of the questions. When you are finished, discuss your answers with a small group of your peers or with the entire class.

EXPLORING THE TEXT

1. What is the main idea or theme of this poem? How do you know?
2. What is the mother's tone as she speaks to her son? How do you know?
3. Why did Hughes choose the title "Mother to Son" instead of referring to stairs in the title?
4. Why did Hughes choose to use informal language in this poem? Does it enhance or detract from your understanding and enjoyment of this poem?

EXPLORING IDEAS

1. Which words and phrases represent the metaphor Hughes uses? (Review your annotations.)
2. When Hughes writes "And sometimes goin' in the dark/Where there ain't been no light," to what might he be referring?
3. What is a "crystal stair"?
4. What metaphor would you use to describe your life?

The New Testament (Book Excerpt)

JAMES McBRIDE

PREREADING

Free write about someone in your family—a parent, a grandparent, a sibling, or a cousin—about whom you have warm memories. You may focus on a specific event or conversation, or you may focus on several memories about this person.

ANNOTATING

While reading, underline any passages that remind you of someone you know, something you have experienced, or some emotion you have felt. In the margins, briefly identify the event, person, or emotion.

Mommy loved God. She went to church each and every Sunday, the only white person in sight, butchering the lovely hymns with a singing voice that sounded like a cross between a cold engine trying to crank on an October morning and a whining Maytag washer. My siblings and I would muffle our laughter as Mommy dug into hymns with a verve and gusto: "*Leaning . . . oh, leannning . . . safe and secure on the—*" Up, up and away she went, her shrill voice climbing higher and higher, reminding us of Curly of the Three Stooges. It sounded so horrible that I often thought Rev. Owens, our minister, would get up from his seat and stop the song. He'd sit behind his pulpit in a spiritual trance, his eyes closed, clad in a long blue robe with a white scarf and billowed sleeves, as if he were prepared to float away to heaven himself, until one of Mommy's clunker notes roused him. One eye would pop open with a jolt, as if someone had just poured cold water down his back. He'd coolly run the eye in a circle, gazing around at the congregation of forty-odd parishioners to see where the whirring noise was coming from. When his eye landed on Mommy, he'd nod as if to say, "Oh, it's just Sister Jordan"; then he'd slip back into his spiritual trance.   (1)

In the real world, Mommy was "Mrs. McBride" or "Mrs. Jordan," depending on whether she used my father's or my stepfather's name, but in Rev. Owens's church, she was Sister Jordan. "Sister Jordan brought quite a few of her children today," Rev. Owens would marvel as Mommy stumbled in with six of us trailing her. "Quite a few." We thought he was hilarious. He was our Sunday school teacher and also the local barber who cut our hair once a month when we grew big enough to refuse Mommy's own efforts in that direction—she literally put a bowl on your head and cut around it. He was a thin man who wore polyester suits and styled his hair in the old slicked-back conk, combed to the back in rippling waves. He could not read very well—I could read better than he could when I was only twelve. He'd stand on the pulpit, handkerchief in hand, wrestling with the Bible verses like a man possessed. He'd begin with, "Our verse for today is . . . ahh . . ." flipping through the pages of his Bible, finally finding the verse, putting his finger on it, and you could hear the clock going *tick, tock, tick, tock,* as he struggled with the words, moving his lips silently while the church waited on edge and my sister Helen, the church pianist, stifled her giggles and Mommy glared at her, shaking her fist and silently promising vengeance once church was over.   (2)

Rev. Owens's sermons started like a tiny choo-choo train and ended up like a roaring locomotive. He'd begin in a slow drawl, then get warmed up and jerk back and forth over the subject matter like a stutterer gone wild: "We . . . [silence] . . . know . . . today . . . arrhh . . . um . . . I said WEEE . . . know . . . THAT [silence] ahhh . . . JESUS [church: "Amen!"] . . . ahhh CAME DOWN . . . ["Yes! Amen!"] I said CAME DOWWWWNNNN! ["Go on!"] He CAME-ON-DOWN-AND-LED-THE-PEOPLE-OF-JERUSALEM-AMEN!" Then he'd shift to a babbling "Amen" mode, where he spoke in a fast motion and the words popped out of his mouth like artillery rounds. "Amens" fired across the room like bullets. "It's so good AMEN to know God AMEN and I tell you AMEN that if you AMEN only come AMEN to God yourself AMEN there will be AMEN no turning back AMEN AMEN AMEN! Can I get an AMEN?" ["AMEN!"]   (3)

And there we were in aisle 5, Sister Jordan in her church hat and blue dress, chuckling and smiling and occasionally waving her hands in the air like everyone else. Mommy loved church. Any church. Even Rev. Owens's Whosoever Baptist Church she loved, though he wasn't her favorite minister because he left his wife, or vice versa—we never knew. Mommy was a connoisseur of ministers; she knew them the way a French wine connoisseur knows Beaujolais red from Vouvray white. Rev. Owens, despite his preaching talents, wasn't even in the top five. That elite list included my late father, the late Rev. W. Abner Brown of Metropolitan Baptist in Harlem, our family friend Rev. Edward Belton, and a few others, all of whom were black, and with the exception of Rev. Belton, quite dead. She considered them old timers, men of dignity and dedication who grew up in the South and remembered what life was like in the old days. They knew how to fire up a church the old-fashioned way, without talk of politics and bad mouthing and negativity but with real talk of God and genuine concern for its parishioners. "Your father," she often mused, "he'd give anybody his last dime." She did not like large churches with political preachers, nor Pentecostal churches that were too wild. And despite her slight dislike of Rev. Owens and his odd style—he once preached a sermon on the word "the"—T-H-E—she had respect for him because his church and preachings were in style to that of her "home" church, New Brown Memorial. Unlike New Brown, however, Whosoever wasn't a storefront church. It was a tiny brick building that stood alone, about fifteen feet back from the sidewalk, with a sign above the door that was done by a painter who began his lettering without taking into account how little space he had. It read: "WHOSOEVER BAPTIST CHURCH."   (4)

I never saw Mommy "get happy" at Whosoever Baptist, meaning "get the spirit" and lose control—thank God. When people got happy it was too much for me. They were mostly women, big mamas whom I knew and loved, but when the good Lord climbed into their bones and lifted them up toward Sweet Liberty, kind gentle women who mussed my hair and kissed me on my cheek and gave me dimes would burst out of their seats like Pittsburgh Steeler linebackers. "Oh *yessss!*" they'd cry, arms outstretched, dancing in the aisles, slithering around with the agility of the Pink Panther, shuddering violently, purse flying one way, hat going another, while some poor old sober-looking deacon tried grimly to hang on to them to keep them from hurting themselves, only to be shaken off like a fly. Sometimes two or three people would physically hold the spirited person to keep her from hurting herself while we looked on in awe, the person convulsing and hollering, "Jesus, Jesus! Yes!" with Rev. Owens winging along with his spirited "AMEN's" and "ah yes's!" I never understood why God would climb into these people with such fervor, until I became a grown man myself and came to understand the nature and power of God's many blessings, but even as a boy I knew God was all powerful because of Mommy's utter deference to Him, and also because she would occasionally do something in church that I never saw her do at home or anywhere else: at some point in the service, usually when the congregation was singing one of her favorite songs, like "We've Come This Far by Faith" or "What a Friend We Have in Jesus," she would bow down her head and weep. It was the only time I ever saw her cry. "Why do you cry in church?" I asked her one afternoon after service.   (5)

"Because God makes me happy."   (6)

"Then why cry?"   (7)

"I'm crying 'cause I'm happy. Anything wrong with that?"   (8)

"No," I said, but there was, because happy people did not seem to cry like she did. Mommy's tears seemed to come from somewhere else, a place far away, a place inside her that she never let any of us children visit, and even as a boy I felt there was a pain behind them. I thought it was because she wanted to be black like everyone else in church, because maybe God like black people better, and one afternoon on the way home from church I asked her whether God was black or white.   (9)

A deep sigh. "Oh boy . . . God's not black. He's not white. He's a spirit."   (10)

"Does he like black or white people better?"   (11)

"He loves all people. He's a spirit."   (12)

"What's a spirit?"   (13)

"A spirit's a spirit."   (14)

"What color is God's spirit?"   (15)

"It doesn't have a color," she said. "God is the color of water. Water doesn't have a color."   (16)

I could buy that, and as I got older I still bought it. . . .   (17)

EXPLORING VOCABULARY

Make a list of three adjectives to describe Mommy. Then get a thesaurus and try to replace each of the entries on your list with an even better adjective.

PROFILING PEOPLE

Using the profile sheet on page 40, write a profile of Mommy. You may have to read between the lines—or make inferences—to answer some of the questions. When you are finished, discuss your answers with a small group of your peers or with the entire class.

EXPLORING THE TEXT

1. Why is this excerpt entitled "The New Testament"?
2. What is McBride's tone?
3. What adjectives does McBride use to describe his mother? How do those adjectives compare with the ones you included on your list?
4. What is the main idea of this passage? Is it implicit or explicit?

EXPLORING IDEAS

1. Why are race and color so important to McBride and his siblings?
2. What challenges do biracial people experience? Does McBride seem to be challenged because he is biracial?
3. What kind of relationship does McBride have with his mother and his brothers?
4. Could you relate personally to anything in this piece? (Review your annotations.)

SUGGESTIONS FOR READING BOOKS ABOUT PEOPLE

The Color of Water by James McBride

Eleni by Nicholas Gage

The Diary of Anne Frank by Anne Frank

SUGGESTIONS FOR SUMMARIZING ESSAYS ABOUT PEOPLE

Choose one of the following works from Unit One and write a summary. Follow the guidelines for summary writing on page 207.

"An Indian Father's Plea: Don't Label My Son a 'Slow Learner'" by Robert Lake

"The Good Daughter" by Caroline Hwang

SUGGESTIONS FOR WRITING ABOUT PEOPLE

1. Interview a person in your class (use the profile sheet as a guide to interviewing and then create your own follow-up questions) and write a letter introducing your classmate to your teacher. Use Robert Lake's letter as a model for your own.

2. Choose someone whose life is very different than yours and interview that person (use the profile sheet as a guide to interviewing and then create your own follow-up questions). You may even want to spend a day with that person in order to observe his or her life. Using the information you've gathered, write a profile of your subject in the form of an essay.

3. Write an essay in which you compare or contrast yourself with a character from one of the readings. It may help to profile yourself by using the profile sheet. Try to focus on significant similarities or differences—not just superficial ones like age, sex, or geographic location.

4. Choose two of the characters about whom you have read who seem very different and write an essay about their similarities. Or choose two characters who seem very similar and write an essay about their differences. Use the profiles you have written as a basis for your essay, but push yourself to study each person more deeply.

5. Write an essay in which you make an assertion about yourself (i.e., "I am unorganized," "I have a bad temper," "I am an eternal optimist," etc.) and support your assertion with examples from your own life.

6. Choose one of the groups to which you belong (religious, social, age, ethnic, racial, or otherwise) and write an essay that profiles that group.

7. Read one of the books listed in this unit and create a profile of the person about whom the book is written or one of the other people in the book. Use the profile sheet to help you gather information about the person you choose. Then write an essay about the person.

PROFILING PEOPLE

Write in the following information about one or more of the people you have read about in Unit One. Remember: The information in some categories may not be directly stated; it may be implied. If it is implied, use clues given by the author to fill in the information. Do not, however, just guess at any given category.

NAME _____

SEX _____

AGE _____

PHYSICAL APPEARANCE _____

LOCATION _____

MARITAL STATUS _____

RACIAL/ETHNIC IDENTITY _____

CULTURAL AFFILIATIONS _____

TRADITIONS _____

VALUES _____

EMPLOYMENT _____

SOCIOECONOMIC CLASS _____

EDUCATIONAL BACKGROUND _____

TALENTS _____

LIKE/DISLIKES _____

FAMILY RELATIONSHIPS _____

OTHER IMPORTANT RELATIONSHIPS _____

PERSONAL CONFLICTS _____

PERSONAL TRIUMPHS _____

UNIT II

PLACES

Po Folks: *Off with Their Heads* (Short Story)

Margo Williams

PREREADING

Free write about one of the most strange or unpleasant jobs you have ever had. If you have never formally worked before, focus on jobs around your house or yard. Share your memories with your classmates.

ANNOTATING

While you read, underline any details about Po Folks that help you get a visual image of the place.

I walk in and the dining room is long with floors made from wide beams of exposed pine. Lined rows of picnic tables are covered in red-and-white checkered plastic tablecloths. The plates look like pounded tin. Iced tea comes in Mason jars without the lids. Waitresses are wearing really short skirts with off-the-shoulder peasant blouses. I cringe when I see the uniforms, and I figure I'd probably have more luck if I'd worn a tight blouse that day. And I figure too, if it hadn't been against the law, Po Folks might just ask their waitresses to serve barefoot.   (1)

They serve huge buckets of hushpuppies and slaw—along with all-you-can-eat fried catfish. Chicken and biscuits and bottomless Mason jars of tea. Crusted over pecan pies and brown pieces of sweet potato pie. The dirty tables are still piled high with greasy bones and stained napkins and lipstick-rimmed coffee cups.   (2)

The place is just some hillbilly-redneck-good-ole-boy concept reinvented by this old Greek guy who is munching on oily black olives and goat cheese when I walk into his office. I play up the S&W Cafeteria job I'd had before, but he just wags his huge head back and forth and says, "We got no waitress openings. Only in the kitchen. Only the kitchen open, but you wouldn't like it. You're too small, too little. Pays good, but you too little."   (3)

I glance out at the dining room and see the way the waitresses laugh real big and shake their long hair back. The way they carry platters of fish around and plop them down on the tables so the men can see down their blouses, and I'm thinking—out back might be a good thing after all, and I sure need some money: "No sir, I'd like the kitchen. The cooking and all. I'm a real hard worker. Don't let my size fool you." Still he doesn't look up from his watery cheese, so I go on with it. "Give me two weeks. Just two weeks and if you don't like me, pay me for one week only."   (4)

Bingo. His fat hands stop grabbing at the olives; he turns and looks me over. After he spits the pits collecting in his cheek into his hand, he laughs. A laugh from way down that shakes his loose belly, and my face is hot, but I hope it isn't too red.   (5)

"You got a deal. I tell you though, little one, I work you hard."

I smile, walk off, promising to return to the second building behind the dining building by seven a.m. on the next Saturday morning, wondering what I've gotten myself into this time. As I walk off he yells, "Wear comfortable shoes, sneakers maybe, or work boots."   (6)

On Saturday morning, the old Greek guy hands me a huge pair of white pants and a white smock-like shirt, and points his flat thumb at a locker room. He tells me to change, clock-in, and pick up a clean rubber apron off the wall opposite the clock. Makes me pull my hair back into a tight bun with two hairnets; the top one is made out of disposable paper with a tight elastic band. Damned uncomfortable things that give me a headache after a couple of hours. He guides me to the second kitchen, which is hardly a kitchen at all. No stoves or way to cook, just big stainless tables, sinks, and a tile floor with open drains. No windows. There are large plastic barrels all over the place and workers stationed at bloody tables.   (7)

The stink of dead fish.   (8)

I look around; I'm the only white working in the kitchen. The old Greek man kind of shakes his head and points to a big black woman, huge back and arms, her smock sleeves rolled up to show giant

muscles. "Nettie her name; she will show you how." He walks off. I
never see him again.   (9)

I walk over to Nettie. I stand behind her feeling tiny, insignificant.
"Excuse me, Ma'am. I'm to be trained by you. Prep girl."   (10)

Nettie doesn't look at me. Pulls out a big catfish, its long whiskers
dangling, a dead eye open and vacant. Slaps it down on a big Lucite
board and gives its head a quick chop with a big heavy knife. She takes
the head and tosses it into one bucket and the body into another.   (11)

Still without looking at me she says, "One chop. Only one chop to
get clean through the head. Howard, he be that old man back there,"
she shrugs her head toward the skinny man standing at the back wall.
"He bring in the fish as fast as you can chop. Somebody else, they
come and bring away the good parts. After you fill a bucket with
heads, you drag them out to the posts out behind the building. The
boys, they'll take it from there. That's it."   (12)

She hands me a knife. The edge scares me; I'm thinking about
bloody fingers coming off. She seems to read my mind. "Don't ever
looks away while you make a chop. Keep you eye on the head."   (13)

Liquid sprays from the fish when the chop comes down hard,
hitting the rubber apron.   (14)

Nettie first laughs at my feeble attempts at the chopping, the head
never completely separating from its body. The sinewy strands keeping
it attached along with my frantic stabbing, stabbing motion. She gets
tired of it after a while though, and keeps on pushing me aside. "No,
no like this. What you want with this fish job? You ain't even got the
strength of a baby in that arm of yours."   (15)

At the end of that first eight-hour shift, I'm finally getting the hang
of it. Nettie says I'll be sorry the next day, but I already am. And, the
next day, back at school with Mora and Lynn, I want to cry telling
them about it. Lynn says, "You can't do that. You've got to quit."   (16)

Mora just keeps on saying, "That's way too gross. Way too gross."
And we hand my flask back and forth in the girls' bathroom, smoking
cigarettes. My right arm aches so badly I can't move it. I keep on using
my left to pick up my bourbon flask. Don't know exactly why I keep
on after that two-week bargain, but I do. Stock pile my money.
Guarding and counting it, planning on taking that money to get clean
away from Mom, away from the Ward, from the sound of those sirens
going off across the street at the hospital. I keep that job for nearly a

month until I throw out my back while lugging a plastic garbage can full of fish heads out to the boys. Can't say I'm completely sorry to have it happen, but laid up on my back at Mom's apartment is no picnic. Mom always nagging about how dumb I was not to ask some boy for help.   (17)

And now I eat fish, but it sure took a long time, and I've sworn off chicken and all other meats for good. I won't touch a fish with whiskers though because you sure don't want to tangle with bottom feeders if you can avoid it.   (18)

EXPLORING VOCABULARY

This passage is an excerpt from a larger work. In paragraph seventeen, the narrator mentions "the Ward." What could she possibly mean here? Is there a way to know without reading the entire work?

PROFILING PLACE

Using the profile sheet on page 76, write a profile of Po Folks. You may have to read between the lines—or make inferences—to answer some of the questions. When you are finished, discuss your answers with a small group of your peers or with the entire class.

EXPLORING THE TEXT

1. Williams uses a number of sentence fragments in this piece. Why does she do so?
2. Which details that the author uses are the most effective? Why? (Review your annotations.)
3. What is the speaker's tone?
4. What is the theme?

EXPLORING ISSUES

1. Why does the narrator prefer to work in the kitchen instead of in the dining room?
2. In paragraph nine, the speaker mentions that she is the only white person working in the kitchen. Why does she mention that? Why doesn't she introduce the race of the waitresses?

3. What does the speaker mean in the last paragraph when she says that ". . . you sure don't want to tangle with the bottom feeders if you can avoid it"?

4. Is this the type of job you could ever hold? Why or why not?

Is There Life on Mars? (TEXTBOOK EXCERPT)

TERESA AUDESIRK AND GERALD AUDESIRK

PREREADING

Do you believe that there is life on other planets or in other galaxies? Upon what evidence do you base your belief?

ANNOTATING

While reading, underline any information that you think might appear on a test if you were reading this for a biology class. In the margins, note why you underlined what you did.

In August 1996, supermarket checkout lines everywhere were lined with tabloids sporting pictures of little green men and doe-eyed aliens that peered out from beneath headlines like "NASA FINDS MARTIANS" and "EXTRATERRESTRIALS FOUND ON MARS!" Even the more conservative media were abuzz with excited pronouncements about life on Mars. What exactly was all the fuss about?   (1)

The excitement and controversy about life on Mars centers, strangely enough, on an object that was found right here on Earth: a softball-sized meteorite that goes by the unassuming name of ALH84001 and was found in 1984 by a meteorite specialist in Antarctica. More than a decade later, other researchers determined that the rock originated on Mars (a determination they reached by comparing the chemical composition of the specimen with that of other meteorites believed to be from Mars). Occasionally, chunks of rock are torn from the Martian surface in the aftermath of collisions with large meteors, and some of this flying debris eventually lands on

Earth. Scientists have thus far found 12 such Martian rocks on Earth, but ALH84001 is by far the oldest piece of Mars found. Radiometric dating puts its age at about 4.5 billion years. This ancient heritage is important, because astronomers believe that the Mars of 4.5 billion years ago was much warmer and wetter than today's cold, barren, dry planet. Perhaps ALH84001 broke away from Mars at a time when conditions were more conducive to life. A team of scientists at NASA, led by David McKay, believe so. They say that the rock of ALH84001 bears evidence that it once held living organisms.   (2)

The McKay team has presented four pieces of evidence in support of their claim that Mars may have supported single-celled organisms in the distant past. (1) The rock contains globules of carbonate that have a structure and chemical composition that suggest they were deposited from an aqueous (water-containing) solution. (2) Many of the carbonate globules are coated with deposits of the minerals iron sulfide and magnetite. Similar deposits of these minerals are made by certain species of bacteria on Earth. (3) ALH84001 contains high levels of chemical substances known as *polycyclic aromatic hydrocarbons* (or PAHs), especially in the vicinity of the carbonate globules. On Earth, PAHs are by-products of biological decomposition. (4) Electron microscopy has revealed the presence of tiny, worm-shaped structures in the meteorite. These structures resemble fossil bacteria that have been found on Earth (though the Mars versions are far smaller than Earth fossils).   (3)

Are the McKay team's findings clear evidence of Martian life? Not really. Skeptics have challenged each of the team's findings, providing convincing evidence that similar features could arise by nonbiological processes or that the meteorite could have been contaminated with terrestrial substances during the 13,000 years that it lay on the Antarctic ice. But the evidence is at the very least suggestive, and biologists, geologists, astronomers, UFO buffs, and other curious humans can't help but be intrigued by these signs that we may not be alone in the universe. Stay tuned.   (4)

EXPLORING VOCABULARY

Study the word parts found on page 203; then underline and define words in this piece that obviously use those word parts. Share your words and definitions with the class.

PROFILING PLACE

Using the profile sheet on page 76, write a profile of Mars. You may have to read between the lines—or make inferences—to answer some of the questions. When you are finished, discuss your answers with a small group of your peers or with the entire class.

EXPLORING THE TEXT

1. Does this textbook excerpt adhere to formal paragraph writing conventions? If so, explain how. If not, how could the paragraphing be improved?
2. Look at the introduction of this piece. Is it effective? Why or why not?
3. What techniques do the authors use to make sure that nonscientists can understand this piece?
4. In paragraph two, the authors use the numerals 1 through 4 to identify four specific points. How could they have done so without using numerals?

EXPLORING IDEAS

1. According to this piece, how does an idea become a fact?
2. What constitutes scientific evidence, and why is evidence important to our belief system?
3. What information in the excerpt might you find on a test if you were reading this for a biology class? (Review your annotations.)
4. What are the four reasons McKay's team believes there was life on Mars? Which reason do you find most compelling?
5. What reasons do the scientists who disagree set forth? Which of their reasons do you find most compelling?
6. Why are human beings so fascinated by the possibility of life on other planets?

Along the Tortilla Curtain (ESSAY)

PETE HAMILL

PREREADING

Look at a map of North, South, and Central America and locate the
countries of the United States, Mexico, Guatemala, El Salvador, Costa
Rica, and Nicaragua. Also locate (on the same map, if possible) the cities
of Tijuana, Mexico; San Ysidro, California; and Oaxaca, Mexico. If possible, refer back to the map as you read the following essay.

ANNOTATING

While reading, underline all the Spanish words, phrases, and sentences
that you encounter. In the margins, write out possible definitions.

You move through the hot, polluted Tijuana morning, past shops and gas
stations and cantinas, past the tourist traps of the Avenida Revolucion,
past the egg-shaped Cultural Center and the new shopping malls and
the government housing with bright patches of laundry hanging on
balconies; then it's through streets of painted adobe peeling in the sun,
ball fields where kids play without gloves, and you see ahead and above
you ten-thousand-odd shacks perched uneasily upon the Tijuana hills,
and you glimpse the green road signs for the beaches as the immense
luminous light of the Pacific brightens the sky. You turn, and along-side
the road there's a chain link fence. It's ten feet high.   (1)

On the other side of the fence is the United States.   (2)

There are wide gashes in the fence, which was once called the
Tortilla Curtain. You could drive three wide loads, side by side, through
the tears in this pathetic curtain. On this morning, on both sides of the
fence (more often called *la linea* by the locals), there are small groups
of young Mexican men dressed in polyester shirts and worn shoes and

faded jeans, and holding small bags. These are a few of the people who are changing the United States, members of a huge army of irregulars engaged in the largest, most successful invasion ever made in North America. (3)

On this day, they smoke cigarettes. They make small jokes. They munch on tacos prepared by a flat-faced, pig-tailed Indian woman whose stand is parked by the roadside. They sip soda. And some of them gaze across the arid scrub and sandy chaparral at the blurred white buildings of the U.S. town of San Ysidro. They wait patiently and do not hide. And if you pull over, and buy a soda from the woman, and speak some Spanish, they will talk. (4)

"I tried last night," says the young man named Jeronimo Vasquez, who wears a Chicago Bears T-shirt under a denim jacket. "But it was too dangerous, too many helicopters last night, too much light. . . ." He looks out at the open stretch of gnarled land, past the light towers at the distant white buildings. "Maybe tonight we will go to Zapata Canyon. . . ." He is from Oaxaca, he says, deep in the hungry Mexican fields; it is now Tuesday, and he starts a job near Stockton on the following Monday, picker's work arranged by his cousin. "I have much time. . . ." (5)

Abruptly, he turns away to watch some action. Two young men are running across the dried scrub on the U.S. side, kicking up little clouds of white dust, while a Border Patrol car goes after them. The young men dodge, circle, running the broken field, and suddenly stand very still as the car draws close. They are immediately added to the cold statistics of border apprehensions. But they are really mere sacrifices; over on the left, three other men run low and hunched, like infantrymen in a fire fight. "Corre, corre," Jeronimo Vasquez whispers. "*Run, run.* . . ." They do. And when they vanish into some distant scrub, he clenches a fist like a triumphant fan. He is not alone. All the others cheer, as does the woman selling tacos, and on the steep hill above the road, a man stands before a tar-paper shack, waves a Mexican flag, and shouts: "*Gol!*" And everyone laughs. (6)

We've all read articles about the 1,950-mile-long border between the United States and Mexico, seen documentaries, heard the bellowing rhetoric of the C-Span politicians enraged at the border's weakness; but until you stand beside it, the border is an abstraction. Up close, you see immediately that the border is at once a concrete place with holes in the fence, and a game, a joke, an affront, a wish, a mere line etched by a draftsman on a map. No wonder George Bush gave up on interdictions as a tactic in the War on Drugs; there are literally hundreds of Ho Chi Minh trails heading into the United States from the south (and others from Canada, of course, and the sea). On some parts of the Mexican border there is one border patrolman for every twenty-six miles; it doesn't require a smuggling genius to figure out how to get twenty tons of cocaine to a Los Angeles warehouse. To fill in the gaps, to guard all the other U.S. borders, would require millions of armed guards, many billions of dollars. And somehow, Jeronimo Vasquez would still appear on a Monday morning in Stockton.   (7)

Those young men beside the ruined fence—not the *narcotraficantes*—are the most typical members of the peaceful invasion. Nobody knows how many come across each year, although in 1988 920,000 were stopped, arrested, and sent back to Mexico by the border wardens. Thousands more make it. Some are described by the outnumbered and overwhelmed immigration police as OTM's (Other Than Mexican, which is to say, Salvadorans, Guatemalans, Nicaraguans, Costa Ricans fleeing war zones, and South Americans and Asians fleeing poverty). Some, like Jeronimo Vasquez, come for a few months, earn money, and return to families in Mexico; others come to stay.   (8)

"When you see a woman crossing," says Jeronimo Vasquez, "you know she's going to stay. It means she has a husband on the other side, maybe even children. She's not going back. Most of the women are from Salvador, not so many Mexicans. . . ."   (9)

Tijuana is one of their major staging grounds. In 1940 it was a town of seventeen thousand citizens, many of whom were employed in providing pleasure for visiting Americans. The clenched, blue-nosed forces of American Puritanism gave the town its function. In 1915 California banned horse racing; dance halls and prostitution were made illegal in 1917; and in 1920 Prohibition became the law of the land. So thousands of Americans began crossing the border to do what they could not do at home: shoot crap, bet on horses, get drunk, and. . . .   (10)

Although commercial sex and good marijuana are still available in Tijuana, sin, alas, is no longer the city's major industry. Today the population is more than one million. City and suburbs are crowded with *maquiladora* plants, assembling foreign goods for export to the United States. These factories pay the highest wages in Mexico (although still quite low by U.S. standards) and attract workers from all over the republic. Among permanent residents, unemployment is very low.   (11)

But it's said that at any given time, one third of the people in Tijuana are transients, waiting to cross to *el otro lado*. A whole subculture that feeds off this traffic can be seen around the Tijuana bus station: coyotes (guides) who for a fee will bring them across; *enganchadores* (labor contractors) who promise jobs; rooming-house operators; hustlers; crooked cops prepared to extort money from the non–Mexicans. The prospective migrants are not simply field hands, making hazardous passage to the valleys of California to do work that even the most poverty-ravaged Americans will not do. Mexico is also experiencing a "skill drain." As soon as a young Mexican acquires a skill or craft—carpentry, wood finishing, auto repair—he has the option of departing for the north. The bags held by some of the young men with Jeronimo Vasquez contained tools. And since the economic collapse of 1982 hammered every citizen of Mexico, millions have exercised the option. The destinations of these young skilled Mexicans aren't limited to the sweatshops of Los Angeles or the broiling fields of the Imperial Valley; increasingly the migrants settle in the cities of the North and East. In New York, I've met Mexicans from as far away as Chiapas, the impoverished state that borders Guatemala. . . .   (12)

The yearly multiplying millions of Mexico will continue moving north unless one of two things happens: the U.S. economy totally collapses, or the Mexican economy expands dramatically. Since neither is likely to happen, the United States of the twenty-first century is certain to be browner, and speak more Spanish, and continue to see its own culture transformed. . . . and in the hills of Tijuana, young men like Jeronimo Vasquez continue to wait for the chance to sprint across the midnight scrub in pursuit of the golden promise of the other side. *Corre, hombre, corre*. . . .   (13)

EXPLORING VOCABULARY

Properly define the Spanish words and phrases in this essay. You may need to consult a Spanish-English dictionary and/or ask someone you know (teacher, friend, or family member) to help you. Then compare the definitions you came up with while reading (review your annotations) with the proper definitions. Consider what clues you relied on to help you formulate your own definitions. Share definitions and clues with your classmates.

PROFILING PLACE

Using the profile sheet on page 76, write a profile of the Tortilla Curtain. You may have to read between the lines—or make inferences—to answer some of the questions. When you are finished, discuss your answers with a small group of your peers or with the entire class.

EXPLORING THE TEXT

1. Why does Hamill use Spanish words and phrases in his essay? How do the phrases add or detract from your reading experience?
2. In this excerpt, Hamill does not directly offer his opinion of illegal immigration. Can you infer his opinion from this excerpt?
3. Hamill's first sentence is very long. Why do you think he chose to use such a long sentence? Is it punctuated correctly?
4. What words, phrases, or sentences do you find particularly effective in describing Tijuana?

EXPLORING ISSUES

1. How do you feel about illegal immigration? What prompts you to feel the way you do?
2. Who decides where a country's border begins and where it ends?
3. What role does poverty play in the immigrants' disregard for immigration laws?
4. What jobs do illegal immigrants do that most Americans will not do? Would you take those jobs if you had to?

A Fable for Tomorrow (Book Excerpt)

RACHEL CARSON

PREREADING

With a small group of your classmates, make a list of all the environmental challenges faced by your neighborhood, your city, your state, or your country. Also brainstorm a list of all the strategies you know of to address those environmental challenges. Share your lists with the rest of the class.

ANNOTATING

While reading, underline any words, phrases, or sentences that help you form a mental picture of what the author is describing.

There was once a town in the heart of America where all life seemed to live in harmony with its surroundings. The town lay in the midst of a checkerboard of prosperous farms, with fields of grain and hillsides of orchards where, in spring, white clouds of bloom drifted above the green fields. In autumn, oak and maple and birch set up a blaze of color that flamed and flickered across a backdrop of pines. Then foxes barked in the hills and deer silently crossed the fields, half hidden in the mists of the fall mornings. (1)

Along the roads, laurel, viburnum and alder, great ferns and wildflowers delighted the traveler's eye through much of the year. Even in winter the roadsides were places of beauty, where countless birds came to feed on the berries and on the seed heads of the dried weeds rising above the snow. The countryside was, in fact, famous for the abundance and variety of its bird life, and when the flood of migrants was pouring through in spring and fall people traveled from great distances to observe them. Others came to fish the streams, which flowed clear and cold out of the hills and contained shady pools where trout lay. So it had been from the days many years ago when the first settlers raised their houses, sank their wells, and built their barns.   (2)

Then a strange blight crept over the area and everything began to change. Some evil spell had settled on the community: mysterious maladies swept the flocks of chickens; the cattle and sheep sickened and died. Everywhere was a shadow of death. The farmers spoke of much illness among their families. In the town the doctors had become more and more puzzled by new kinds of sickness appearing among their patients. There had been several sudden and unexplained deaths, not only among adults but even among children, who would be stricken suddenly while at play and die within a few hours.   (3)

There was a strange stillness. The birds, for example—where had they gone? Many people spoke of them, puzzled and disturbed. The feeding stations in the backyard were deserted. The few birds seen anywhere were moribund; they trembled violently and could not fly. It was spring without voices. On the mornings that had once throbbed with the dawn chorus of robins, catbirds, doves, jays, wrens, and scores of other bird voices there was now no sound; only silence lay over the fields and woods and marsh.   (4)

On the farms the hens brooded, but no chicks hatched. The farmers complained that they were unable to raise any pigs—the litters were small and the young survived only a few days. The apple trees were coming into bloom but no bees droned among the blossoms, so there was no pollination and there would be no fruit.   (5)

The roadsides, once so attractive, were now lined with browned and withered vegetation as though swept by fire. These, too, were silent, deserted by all living things. Even the streams were now lifeless. Anglers no longer visited them, for all the fish had died.   (6)

In the gutters under the eaves and between the shingles of the roofs, a white granular powder still showed a few patches; some weeks before it had fallen like snow upon the roofs and the lawns, the fields and the streams.   (7)

No witchcraft, no enemy action had silenced the rebirth of new life in this stricken world. People had done it themselves.   (8)

This town does not actually exist, but it might easily have a thousand counterparts in America or elsewhere in the world. I know of no community that has experienced all the misfortunes I describe. Yet every one of these disasters has actually happened somewhere, and many real communities have already suffered a substantial number of them. A grim specter has crept upon us almost unnoticed, and this imagined tragedy may easily become a stark reality we all shall know. . . .   (9)

EXPLORING VOCABULARY

With a small group of your classmates, choose one of the paragraphs in this piece, reread it, and underline all the words with which you are unfamiliar or that you cannot readily define. Then look up each word in the dictionary, and choose the definition which best fits the meaning for the sentence. Present your findings to the class.

PROFILING PLACE

Using the profile sheet on page 76, write a profile of the earth. You may have to read between the lines—or make inferences—to answer some of the questions. When you are finished, discuss your answers with a small group of your peers or with the entire class.

EXPLORING THE TEXT

1. Why does Carson choose to write this chapter from her book as a story instead of an essay or an article? Is this story format effective? Why or why not?
2. Carson uses a great deal of description is this piece. Which descriptions do you find to be the most effective? Why? (Review your annotations.)
3. Does Carson use a specific strategy to compare and contrast the different states of the town she describes? If so, what is her strategy?
4. What is the main idea of this chapter?

EXPLORING IDEAS

1. This piece was published in 1966. Do you think that America's environmental problems have worsened since then? Explain.
2. Do you know of a place that has recently suffered from environmental destruction? Describe the problems.

3. Carson suggests that "this imagined tragedy may easily become a stark reality we all shall know." Do you agree with her? Why or why not?
4. What specific actions can you take in your daily life to help preserve the environment?

In the Suburbs (POEM)

LOUIS SIMPSON

PREREADING

With a small group of your classmates, define the word *suburb*. Then identify the suburbs in your city or town. Who lives there? Share your answers with the class.

ANNOTATING

While reading, put a slash (/) after each sentence. In the margins, write what you think each sentence means.

> There's no way out.
> You were born to waste your life.
> You were born to this middleclass life.
>
> As others before you
> Were born to walk in procession   (5)
> To the temple, singing.

EXPLORING VOCABULARY

What is the difference among the terms lower class, upper class, and middle class? You may want to look in a dictionary and then move to a reference book like an encyclopedia to find the answer. Share your findings with the class.

PROFILING PLACE

Using the profile sheet on page 76, write a profile of the suburbs. You may have to read between the lines—or make inferences—to answer some of the questions. When you are finished, discuss your answers with a small group of your peers or with the entire class.

EXPLORING THE TEXT

1. How many sentences make up this poem? (Review your annotations.)
2. What is the theme?
3. Why did the author divide such a short poem into two separate stanzas?

EXPLORING ISSUES

1. To what does the speaker compare middle-class life? (Review your annotations.)
2. What is the speaker's attitude toward the suburbs? How do you know?
3. Do you agree with the speaker's characterization of the suburbs? Why or why not?

The House on Mango Street (NOVEL EXCERPT)

SANDRA CISNEROS

PREREADING

In a free write, describe your dream house. Be very specific about the features you want your dream house to include. Share your description with your classmates.

ANNOTATING

While reading, underline any words, phrases, or sentences that tell you how the narrator feels about the places she has lived. In the margins, write an adjective to describe those feelings.

We didn't always live on Mango Street. Before that we lived on Loomis on the third floor, and before that we lived on Keeler. Before Keeler it was Paulina, and before that I can't remember. But what I remember most is moving a lot. Each time it seemed there'd be one more of us. By the time we got to Mango Street, we were six—Mama, Papa, Carlos, Kiki, my sister Nenny and me.　(1)

The house on Mango Street is ours, and we don't have to pay rent to nobody, or share the yard with the people downstairs, or be careful not to make too much noise, and there isn't a landlord banging on the ceiling with a broom. But even so, it's not the house we'd thought we'd get.　(2)

We had to leave the flat on Loomis quick. The water pipes broke and the landlord wouldn't fix them because the house was too old. We had to leave fast. We were using the washroom next door and carrying water over in empty milk gallons. That's why Mama and Papa looked for a house, and that's why we moved into the house on Mango Street, far away, on the other side of town. (3)

They always told us that one day we would move into a house, a real house that would be ours for always so we wouldn't have to move each year. And our house would have running water and pipes that worked. And inside it would have real stairs, not hallway stairs, but stairs inside like the houses on T.V. And we'd have a basement and at least three washrooms so when we took a bath we wouldn't have to tell everybody. Our house would be white with trees around it, a great big yard and grass growing without a fence. This was the house Papa talked about when he held a lottery ticket and this was the house Mama dreamed up in the stories she told us before we went to bed. (4)

But the house on Mango Street is not the way they told it at all. It's small and red with tight steps in front and windows so small you'd think they were holding their breath. Bricks are crumbling in places, and the front door is so swollen you have to push hard to get in. There is no front yard, only four little elms the city planted by the curb. Out back is a small garage for the car we don't own yet and a small yard that looks smaller between the two buildings on either side. There are stairs in our house, but they're ordinary hallway stairs, and the house has only one washroom. Everybody has to share a bedroom—Mama and Papa, Carlos and Kiki, me and Nenny. (5)

Once when we were living on Loomis, a nun from my school passed by and saw me playing out front. The Laundromat downstairs had been boarded up because it had been robbed two days before and the owner had painted on the wood YES WE'RE OPEN so as not to lose business. (6)

Where do you live? she asked. (7)

There, I said pointing up to the third floor. (8)

You live *there*? (9)

There. I had to look where she pointed—the third floor, the paint peeling, wooden bars Papa had nailed on the windows so we wouldn't fall out. You live *there*? The way she said it made me feel like nothing. *There.* I lived *there.* I nodded. (10)

I knew then I had to have a house. A real house. One I could point to. But this isn't it. The house on Mango Street isn't it. For the time being, Mama says. Temporary, says Papa. But I know how those things go. (11)

EXPLORING VOCABULARY

Using a thesaurus, look up the word *house* and write down as many synonyms as you can find that would be appropriate substitutes in the title of this piece. Remember that *house* is used as a noun in the title. Does the narrator use any of these synonyms? Why or why not?

PROFILING PLACE

Using the profile sheet on page 76, write a profile of the house on Mango Street. You may have to read between the lines—or make inferences—to answer some of the questions. When you are finished, discuss your answers with a small group of your peers or with the entire class.

EXPLORING THE TEXT

1. What is the narrator's tone?
2. How old do you think the narrator is? Why?
3. Why do you think the author chose not to use quotation marks when writing dialogue?
4. What specific points does the narrator use to compare the house on Mango Street with the house that "Papa talked about when he held a lottery ticket"?

EXPLORING IDEAS

1. How does the narrator feel about the places she has lived? (Review your annotations.)
2. Why is a certain kind of house so important to the narrator? What does it represent?
3. Where do you currently live? How do you feel about living there?
4. The narrator ends this piece with the sentence: "But I know how those things go." What does she mean?

What We Can Learn from Japan's Prisons (ESSAY)

JAMES WEBB

PREREADING

With your classmates, read the Bill of Rights contained within the U.S. Constitution. Identify the ones intended to protect the rights of those accused or convicted of crimes. Discuss whether you think these rights are valuable or not. Explain your opinion.

ANNOTATING

While you are reading, underline any ideas that seem to contradict the rights guaranteed in the Bill of Rights. In the margins, identify which right is being contradicted.

Fuchu Prison, near Tokyo, is home to 2500 of Japan's most hardened criminals. Ed Arnett is an alumnus who thinks of Fuchu daily. The dank, unheated buildings, the harshness of the guards' reports to their superiors, the high stone walls—these are as near to him as the scars on his legs, from the frostbite he picked up in his Fuchu cell. (1)

"I didn't know I could still cry until I went to prison in Japan," says Arnett, convicted in 1979 for possession of two kilograms of marijuana. "I wouldn't put that experience on anybody." (2)

Arrested on Okinawa, Arnett was kept in pretrial confinement for a month. He endured days of intense interrogation without an attorney and signed a confession—written in Japanese—that he could not read. He met his lawyer for the first time at his trial. The trial took thirty minutes. He was not allowed a jury. (3)

At Fuchu, Arnett lived in a 9-by-5-foot cell furnished with a hard, narrow bed, a sink that also was his desk and a toilet that he could flush only when permitted by the guards. His mail was censored, and he was not allowed writing materials. The books he read were the few approved by his guards. Gifts from home were kept from him until his release. Despite his diabetes, Arnett's diet was dominated by seaweed, fish and rice. He lost 55 pounds in 18 months. Fourteen of those months were spent in solitary, in a room where a television camera recorded his every move. His scalp was shaved every two weeks. He was forbidden to look out the window or to communicate with other inmates. He worked eight hours a day, even in solitary, making paper bags in his cell. He could not touch his bunk during the day, but when the lights went out at night, if he was not lying down, he was punished. On his release, due to improper treatment of his diabetes, an American doctor called him "a walking dead man."   (4)

Arnett's experiences were not unusual for Japanese prison inmates, about 100 of whom at any time are Americans serving sentences for crimes ranging from minor drug offenses to murder. But, surprisingly, Arnett, home in Nebraska, says he prefers Japan's legal system to ours. Why? "Because it's fair," he says. "The Japanese never tried to trick me, even in interrogation. They were always trustworthy. I could have got five years, and they gave me two. The Americans who were helping them wanted me to get 20. The guards at Fuchu were hard, but they never messed with you unless there was a reason. You didn't have to worry about other prisoners coming after you, either. And the laws of Japan are for everybody. That's the main thing. The laws in this country depend on how much you can pay. I'd rather live under a hard system that's fair."   (5)

In 1981, Japan, with about half our population, had only 922 homicides; we had 1832 in New York City alone. An American is 12 times more likely to be murdered than a Japanese, 14 times more likely to be raped and 20 times more likely to be a victim of a property crime. Although recidivism rates are similar—50 percent in Japan, 64 percent here—our problem with criminal repeaters is actually nine times greater than Japan's because our crime rate is so much higher.   (6)

A defendant's lack of counsel during interrogation and the absence of a jury trial, a U.S. Constitutional right, raises no hackles. "There are scholars who criticize this, but they have no social or political support," notes Kotaro Ohno of Japan's Ministry of Justice, who studied law at Harvard. "A Japanese believes the judge is more knowledgeable about his situation than a collection of citizens." Ohno defends Japan's very narrow use of the exclusionary rule and says the U.S. "goes too far" in excluding illegally obtained evidence. (7)

Japan has a low crime rate without either a police state or excessive litigation. Only 50,000 prisoners, including pretrial detention inmates, are presently confined in Japan, and fewer than 4 percent of the prisoners are sentenced for longer than three years. In the U.S., there are 580,000 adult inmates, and 80 percent of those in state institutions have been sentenced for longer than five years. (8)

Observes Yoshio Suzuki, until recently director of the Correction Bureau in Japan's Ministry of Justice: "The law in Japan is severe in the attitude toward offenders as a whole. This allows it to be lenient in the punishment of the individual. We involve the victim in the criminal process. If the accused has shown proper grief, and the victim tells this to the court, it will go much easier on the accused." (9)

Japan brings 70 percent of its crimes to conviction. The U.S. brings only 19.8 percent of its crimes to arrest. But the contrast in prisons themselves is most startling. Americans familiar with the horrors of Attica and New Mexico and the routine tales of brutality and homosexual rape would find the orderly corridors of a Japanese prison mind-boggling. (10)

"They don't coddle them, but they don't abuse them, either," says U. S. Navy Capt. Everette Stumbaugh, a lawyer for the commander of U. S. forces in Japan. "Japan plays it aboveboard all the way." (11)

There never has been a hostage crisis in a Japanese prison. There has been only one "prison disturbance"—30 years ago. There never has been a reported case of homosexual rape, or of prisoner gang wars. No guard has ever been killed by inmates: there has been only one inmate death in the last 10 years at the hands of another. There have been only 35 escapes from Japanese prisons in the last seven years (the U.S. average is more than 8000 escapes a year). Almost 94 percent of Japan's prisoners perform labor that is geared to their aptitude and rehabilitative potential, rather than based on the crime committed. Guards typically are unarmed. There are 58 major prisons in Japan. In addition to Fuchu, I toured prisons in Yokosuka and Okinawa. Only Fuchu had armed guards. There, fewer than 10 percent carry weapons—police sticks. (12)

"What about the guard in the tower?" I asked Kaoru Kayaba, Yokosuka's warden, as I stared at the juncture of two walls on the far side of a large athletic field. "Doesn't he carry a rifle?" (13)

Kayaba smiled. "We don't keep a guard in the tower. Except when the prisoners play softball." (14)

"In case a prisoner vaults the wall?" (15)

"In case a ball goes over the wall." (16)

Much of the success of Japan's prisons is due to a classification system that analyzes and separates hardened criminals ("Category B") from those not likely to become repeat offenders ("Category A"). Yokosuka and Okinawa house "A" prisoners. The A's often earn certificates in trades such as plastering and auto repair. The B's—many of whom are members of the *Yakuza*, Japan's Mafia—might do such mundane tasks as maintenance work or making toys. (17)

Prison officials are highly trained. Last year, though two-thirds of those who passed the national qualifying test for prison guards were university graduates, only one-fourth were hired. Successful applicants must spend two weeks as observers in a prison and then complete eight months of intense training before they may begin work. Guards are transferred every few years to promote standardization within the system. (18)

All Japanese wardens began as guards. Their experiences have given them both "hands on" time with prisoners and philosophical depth. Yokosuka's Warden Kayaba affirms the good of man. "All human beings are 98 percent good and 2 percent bad," he says. "The men who end up in prison are not more evil than others in our society. They are weaker. With the proper education, we can make even the worst offenders as calm as the others." Guards do this not through force, but through intense counseling and psychical denial. A difficult prisoner is removed from the collective environment and placed in an even more austere "punishment cell," where counseling continues. "We make them think," says Kayaba. "We talk to them again and again about why they were sent to prison, until gradually they understand." (19)

"We are their caretakers, not their oppressors," says Fuchu's present warden, Kiyoshi Taru, of Japan's most hardened criminals. An aircraft gunner during World War II, Taru saw the corrections field as a way to continue serving his country after Japan's military was disbanded.

"Criminals have violated the well-being of others in order to satisfy their greed," says Taru. "We teach them how to control their desires and still satisfy themselves. You cannot do this unless you are unimpeachable yourself. We use our example as the instrument for their rehabilitation." (20)

Taru says all guards are martial arts experts but adds, "If a guard unfairly strikes a prisoner, he will himself be imprisoned for a mandatory seven-year sentence." (21)

Okinawa's warden, Yoshitaka Myojin, followed his father into the field. He says the key to prison stability lies in the workshop: "The guard who runs the workshop performs three functions—instructor, disciplinarian, and counselor—so the prisoner does not direct his anger toward the guard purely as an authority figure. The guard is part of the overall unit, the father figure." Noting with irony that many fundamentals of the Japanese system were adapted from the U.S. system, Myojin wonders, "What has happened in America?" (22)

His question is echoed by many here. If the U.S. incarceration rate is one of the highest in the free world, so is its crime rate. Overcrowding—our prison population has expanded by 30 percent in the last three years—contributes to abuse and acts of violence. So does idleness. Few prisoners work in U.S. jails because of trade-union pressure and "state use" laws that forbid their making competitive products. Only about 10 percent of the inmates in our state system are allowed to work. (23)

Our guards are often unskilled and untrained. Robert Fosen, director of the Commission on Accreditation for Corrections, indicates that the "recommended levels of training" that his group recently set for U.S. prisons consist of a mere 40 hours of "orientation training," followed during the guard's first year by 120 hours of further training in supervision and the use of force. He notes that standards had to rise "in well over half the states" to meet these new requirements. (24)

Could we adopt parts of the Japanese system? I asked three Americans of markedly differing political views and responsibilities: Norman Carlson, director of the Federal Bureau of Prisons since 1970, who inspected the Japanese system in 1971; Fosen, who was a New York prison official during the Attica riots; and Edward Koren, an attorney for the American Civil Liberties Union's National Prison Project. (25)

All three support more inmates working, and Carlson and Fosen favor a decrease in the length of sentences for nonviolent, nondangerous offenders but longer sentences for others.   (26)

Carlson notes that all federal wardens begin as line officers. Fosen argues that our varied institutions require a wider range of training. Koren agrees.   (27)

Their greatest resistance to the Japanese system concerns individual treatment. Says Koren: "No heat in a prisoner's cell is outrageous. That would be a clear violation of the Constitution's prohibition against cruel and unusual punishment. The other living conditions are quite extreme. The denial of reading materials without clearly showing they are a threat to prison order, the withholding of writing materials from inmates and the censorship of correspondence all violate the First Amendment." He suggests many of Japan's methods would end in U.S. lawsuits.   (28)

Koren says of Japanese trial procedures: "The exclusionary rule is our way of enforcing Constitutional rights. Involving the victim *before* a person is convicted should be done only at the defendant's initiative. Eliminating plea bargaining would be impractical."   (29)

But is the present U.S. way fair?   (30)

"American jails are filled with hate," says Arnett. "If their walls fell down today, do you think the prisoners would run past you without stopping? An American prisoner might kill you just because you're the first person he sees. If the walls of the Japanese prisons fell down, the Japanese prisoners would just go home."   (31)

I told this to Toyofumi Yoshinaga, a legal assistant at the Correction Bureau in Tokyo who had spent several hours providing me with statistics. His eyes lit up. Said Yoshinaga: "During the great Kanto earthquake of 1923, the walls of one of our prisons *did* fall down." He smiled. "No one escaped."   (32)

EXPLORING VOCABULARY

Using context clues (see page 200) and/or word parts (see page 203), define the following words: recidivism (paragraph six), coddle (paragraph eleven), mundane (paragraph seventeen), psychical (paragraph nineteen), unimpeachable (paragraph twenty).

PROFILING PLACE

Using the profile sheet on page 76, write a profile of a Japanese prison. You may have to read between the lines—or make inferences—to answer some of the questions. When you are finished, discuss your answers in a small group of your peers or with the entire class.

EXPLORING THE TEXT

1. Why does the author use so many statistics? Are they effective?
2. What is Webb's main point?
3. Who is Webb's intended audience?
4. Webb uses quite a few quotes. How do these quotes enhance his point?

EXPLORING IDEAS

1. What are the major differences between each type of prison? What are the similarities?
2. In paragraph nineteen, Webb quotes Warden Kayaba who says, "All human beings are 98 percent good and 2 percent bad. . . ." Do you agree or disagree? Why?
3. Reread paragraph twenty-eight. Do you agree that the absence of heat in prison cells and the controlling of prisoners' reading and writing materials violate prisoners' rights? (Review your annotations.)
4. Which prison would you prefer? Why?

Familiar Footing (ESSAY)

CHERYL SABA

PREREADING

Free write about something you cannot seem to resist; it could be a certain food, a certain kind of clothing, or a certain kind of activity. Consider why you have such a hard time resisting.

ANNOTATING

While reading, underline any descriptive details that you find particularly effective. In the margins, briefly note why.

That's the one.   (1)

I never would have guessed that what I have been yearning for all this time would appear before my eyes only moments after crossing the threshold of this fine establishment. I know I've been particular in the past, and I haven't really been the type to settle. Now is not the time to let an opportunity like this pass me by. It has been a long time, after all.   (2)

I see them all; they are too numerous to take in quickly, but I can't let this one get away. Though I do want to look around a bit more. After all, I prepared myself for a long visit. The expected doesn't distract me: the dim lighting, strangers meandering around the room, eye-contact being made in between sets. But the silhouette beckoning to me from the rear of the room maintains my attention. Initial contact has been made.   (3)

Despite the multitude of enticing, red velvet chairs I pass—some occupied by the discriminating patron, others empty and beckoning for the next passer-by looking for the right angle—I am focused.   (4)

Why do my eyes continue to be drawn to that one?   (5)

Well, perfect size and shape are a must. Certainly no lack here. Just the right height; perfect for dancing on those long, romantic evenings, or maybe just a spontaneous stroll in the park after dinner. And those shapely, sinuous curves—all in the right places and perfectly toned. Looks like a perfect fit from here, but I don't want to seem too anxious. I can't help but notice others looking in the same direction, but the signals they are giving off seem to lack the intensity I feel, which must be visible to even the most casual observer. How can I resist, especially considering it's been so very long since I've done this sort of thing?   (6)

People always warn me that I should be more careful in these matters based on the mistakes I've made in the past. Stop being impulsive, they tell me. You've got too much at risk, they warn.   (7)

I need a closer look.   (8)

I knew I would smell that familiar scent wafting through the air if I dared to approach. I can identify it immediately. It's the real thing— fresh, strong, smart, sensible, all wrapped into one, if that's possible. Enticing me even further is the hue. How can I describe it in a way to do proper justice? A healthy blend of island-tropic tan with touches of light beige where the sun don't shine (so to speak). The illumination from the overhead track lighting reflects a slight shimmer, adding to the appeal.   (9)

Tall, dark and handsome all right.   (10)

I wonder if I can afford to risk what I have in the hopes that I'll get what I need in return. I haven't even really considered my options. I look around and spy three to the right, two more to the left, and a couple over in the corner by the proprietor, who is attending to those in need of assistance. As I pass people by, I can hear the typical lines being exchanged—nothing new here. Everyone is playing the game, hoping to leave with what they came in for—nothing more, nothing less. I guess I'm no different, though there is no telling what may come out of my mouth once I reach what I've clearly set my sights on.   (11)

It seems as though they are on display, just for my eyes to feast on, but maybe that's because I've only got one thing on mind at this point. Something tells me I need to slow down, take a deep breath, and get things into perspective. This is not the type of thing to be taken lightly. I've made so many mistakes in the past—I don't want to make any more.   (12)

Either the walls are closing in, or something beyond my control is
bringing me closer.   (13)

Throw caution to the wind.   (14)

"Hi there."   (15)

"Hello." Great, now is my chance.   (16)

"You seem interested. Am I right?"   (17)

"I'm sorry. Was I being that obvious?" (Maybe I should bat my
eyelashes a bit.)   (18)

"Don't worry. I've grown used to it!"   (19)

Suddenly, I feel nervous and my palms begin to sweat. "I can't do
this. I need to leave," I shriek.   (20)

I've got to get out of here before I do something I may regret. I just
hope I don't collide with one of the golden horns on the way out the door. (21)

"Wait . . . I know what you want, and I think you've made the right
choice."   (22)

Somebody seems to know me already.   (23)

"But I'm afraid of what will it cost me."   (24)

"Don't worry. Trust me."   (25)

Now I feel faint, but I listen. My knees weaken and my heart
pounds as we gaze into each other's eyes. Glancing quickly towards the
exit, I notice it's getting dark outside, making the flashing neon sign
hanging just beyond the entrance even more ominous.   (26)

"I don't have too much to give at this point, but I can afford to
hand over the better part of what I do have—for the sake of a good
investment, of course."   (27)

"Sounds reasonable."   (28)

Staring into each other's eyes, I find it hard to believe I am making
this kind of sacrifice on the turn of a dime, literally. But I'm not strong
enough to turn away . . .   (29)

Once the exchange is over and I glide through the double glass
doors out into the nearly-vacant parking lot, I expect somehow to feel
empty, but I don't. I've just made one of the best decisions of my life.   (30)

Sixty-five dollars is a damn good deal on an Italian-made leather
pair of stiletto heels!   (31)

EXPLORING VOCABULARY

In paragraph twenty-nine, Saba uses the expression "on the turn of a dime." What does that mean? Share your answer with the class.

PROFILING PLACES

Using the profile sheet on page 76, write a profile of the establishment Saba describes. You may have to read between the lines—or make inferences—to answer some of the questions. When you are finished, discuss your answers with a small group of your peers or with the entire class.

EXPLORING THE TEXT

1. How does the dialogue enhance Saba's essay?
2. Which descriptive details do you think are most effective? (Review your annotations.)
3. What is Saba's purpose?

EXPLORING IDEAS

1. What kind of place is Saba describing?
2. In paragraph twenty-one, Saba writes, "I just hope I don't collide with one of the golden horns on the way out the door." What are the golden horns?
3. Were you surprised by the ending? Why? What kind of place did you think Saba was describing?

SUGGESTIONS FOR READING BOOKS ABOUT PLACES

The House on Mango Street by Sandra Cisneros

Blue Highways by William Least Heat-Moon

The Good Earth by Pearl S. Buck

SUGGESTIONS FOR SUMMARIZING ESSAYS ABOUT PLACES

Choose one of the following works from Unit Two and write a summary. Follow the guidelines for summary writing on page 207.

"What We Can Learn from Japan's Prisons" by James Webb

"Along the Tortilla Curtain" by Pete Hamill

SUGGESTIONS FOR WRITING ABOUT PLACES

1. Write an essay that describes your home and what it means to you. Use the profile sheet in this unit to help you gather information.
2. With a group of your classmates, write a travel brochure about your city or town. Be sure to review brochures on other cities or towns before you begin.
3. Write an essay in which you discuss how your life would be different if you were born in another place. For example, if you were born in a small village in the South American rainforest, how would your life be different? You may need to do some research reading before you begin this essay.
4. Write an essay about how the city, town, neighborhood, country, state, street, or home you live in has shaped you as a person.
5. Choose two of the places described in this unit and write an essay in which you compare or contrast them. Use the profile sheet in this unit to help you gather information on each place. Then begin to compare or contrast. Do not focus on just the obvious; dig more deeply.
6. Watch the film *Pleasantville* and write an essay about how the town changes and why the town changes.
7. Read one of the books listed and then write an essay profiling the place being written about. Use the profile sheet in this unit to help you gather information.
8. Write about a place that gives you comfort or solace and explain why it does.

PROFILING PLACES

Fill in the following information about one or more of the places you have read about in Unit Two. Remember that the information in some categories may not be directly stated; it may be implied. If it is implied, use clues given by the author to infer the answer. Remember also that the information in some categories may not be directly stated or implied, so do not just guess at any given category.

NAME _____

PURPOSE OR FUNCTION _____

GEOGRAPHIC LOCATION _____

APPEARANCE/LAY-OUT _____

DISTINGUISHING CHARACTERISTICS _____

LANDMARKS _____

HISTORY _____

SIGNIFICANT CHANGES
IN APPEARANCE, FUNCTION,
POPULATION, ETC. _____

TYPE(S) OF PEOPLE WHO LIVE
OR WORK OR VISIT _____

NUMBER OF PEOPLE WHO LIVE
OR WORK OR VISIT _____

ACTIVITIES _____

PEOPLE'S ATTITUDE ABOUT THE PLACE _____

INFLUENCE ON PEOPLE'S LIVES _____

CONFLICTS ASSOCIATED
WITH PLACE _____

TRIUMPHS ASSOCIATED
WITH PLACE _____

Unit III

EVENTS

Taunting of a Suicidal Woman Shocks Seattle

Residents Search Their Souls After Drivers in Traffic Jam Yell "Jump" at Bridge Leaper (NEWSPAPER ARTICLE)

PATRICK MCMAHON

PREREADING

Free write about a time that someone—or a group of people—taunted you. (You may need to look up the word *taunt* in a dictionary.) How did it make you feel? How did you respond?

ANNOTATING

While reading, underline any words, passages, or phrases that evoke a strong feeling in you. In the margins, write down the name of the feeling you experience.

In a city once best-known for its laid-back charm, people are grappling with reports that motorists taunted a woman threatening suicide on a bridge. (1)

Radio talk shows and coffeehouses buzzed with opinions Wednesday. Morning news programs featured it. A public radio station here devoted an hour to the topic "Civility in the City," and the city's mood, psyche, and notorious traffic were topic A. (2)

"I think the initial reaction is shock: that this is not what we're really about," said Ross Reynolds, KUOW public radio host. "And then there were people who said this is exactly what we're about and what traffic has done to us." (3)

"The biggest response is the incredible soul-searching that is going on," civic activist Ref Lindmark said. "People want to know whatever happened to 'Seattle nice.'" (4)

The incident occurred Tuesday morning on Interstate 5—the major north-south thoroughfare through Seattle. Traffic was tied up for four hours. Police initially shut down only part of the bridge to assist the 26-year-old woman, who threatened to jump 160 feet into Lake Union. But once passing motorists and bus passengers began shouting catcalls and obscenities at the woman they closed down the entire span at 8 a.m.   (5)

"People were yelling, 'Jump, bitch, jump!' " Seattle police spokesman Clem Benton said. "Now, who wants to hear that in this type of situation?"   (6)

"I was appalled," Assistant Police Chief John Diaz said. "Every once in a while, I forget that Seattle isn't the quaint little burb it used to be."   (7)

The woman jumped at about 10 a.m. She survived—and is hospitalized in serious condition at Harborview Medical Center, where dozens of bouquets were delivered Wednesday from the public. *The Seattle Times* identified the woman as a lobbyist distraught over a relationship.   (8)

By several indicators, Seattle has some of the most congested roads in America. "You can see how frayed people's nerves are in this town about traffic," said David Brewster, former editor of *Seattle Weekly*. "Not that anyone will vote money to solve it."   (9)

Wednesday morning, radio reaction was non-stop. "We planned on giving it 2 hours, and it went for 4," said Kirby Wilbur, conservative host of a morning drive-time show on KVI-AM. "The big majority of calls were ashamed of the people doing the catcalls.   (10)

The national attention frustrated some he said. "It's another blow to our image" after the World Trade organization protests in 1999, the Mardi Gras rioting that left one person dead earlier this year and the loss of the Boeing's headquarters this spring.   (11)

The incident was reminiscent of a suicide attempt in 1998 on the Woodrow Wilson Bridge outside Washington, D.C., that tied up traffic for several hours.   (12)

EXPLORING VOCABULARY

Find the word *burb* in paragraph seven. Using context clues (see page 200) try to define the word. Share your findings with the class.

PROFILING EVENTS

Using the profile sheet on page 114, write a profile of this event. You may have to read between the lines—or make inferences—to address some of the categories. When you are finished, discuss your answers with a small group of your peers or with the entire class.

EXPLORING THE TEXT

1. How would this piece be different if it were an essay instead of a newspaper article?
2. The author uses very short paragraphs. Why?
3. Why does McMahon use so many quotes?

EXPLORING IDEAS

1. What feelings did you experience as you read this article? (Review your annotations.)
2. Have you ever gotten so angered by a traffic incident that you behaved in a mean way to someone else?
3. Do you think that Seattle's frustrating traffic conditions explain the motorists' behavior? If so, why? If not, explain their behavior.

Dreaming: Mysterious Mental Activity During Sleep (Textbook Excerpt)

Samuel L. Wood and Ellen Green Wood

PREREADING

In a free write, describe the most memorable dream that you have ever had.

ANNOTATING

While you are reading, underline any information that could help you interpret or understand the dream you described in your free write. In the margins, note how what you underlined relates to your dream.

People have always been fascinated by dreams. The vivid dreams people remember and talk about are **REM dreams**—the type that occur almost continuously during each REM period. But people also have **NREM dreams,** dreams that occur during NREM sleep, although they are typically less frequent and less memorable than REM dreams (Foulkes, 1996). REM dreams have a storylike or dreamlike quality and are more visual, vivid, and emotional than NREM dreams (Hobson, 1989). Blind people who lose their sight before age 5 usually do not have visual dreams. Nevertheless, they have vivid dreams involving other senses.

(1)

You may have heard that an entire dream takes place in an instant. Do you find that hard to believe? In fact, it is not true. Sleep researchers have discovered that it takes about as long to dream a dream as it would to experience the same thing in real life (Kleitman, 1960). Let's take a closer look at the dream state.

(2)

Dream Memories: We Remember Only a Few

Although some people insist that they do not dream at all, sleep researchers say that all people dream unless they are drinking heavily or taking drugs that suppress REM sleep. Sleepers have the best recall of a dream if they are awakened during the dream; the more time that passes after the dream ends, the poorer the recall. If you awaken 10 minutes or more after the dream ends, you will probably not remember it. Even the dreams you remember on awakening will quickly fade from memory unless you mentally rehearse them or write them down. Very few dreams are memorable enough to be retained very long. Some researchers suggest that human brain chemistry during sleep differs from that in the waking state and does not facilitate the storing of memories (Hobson, 1996; Hobson & Stickgold, 1995).   (3)

   Would people be better off if they remembered more of their dreams? Probably not. If dream memories were as vivid as memories of real events, people might have difficulty differentiating between events that actually happened and those they merely dreamed about.   (4)

The Content of Dreams: Bizarre or Commonplace?

What do people dream about? You may be surprised to learn that dreams are less bizarre and less filled with emotion than is generally believed (Cipolli et al., 1993; Hall & Van de Castle, 1996; Snyder, 1971). Because dreams are notoriously hard to remember, the features that stand out tend to be those that are bizarre or emotional.   (5)

   Sleep researchers generally agree that dreams reflect a person's preoccupations in waking life—hopes and plans, worries and fears. Most dreams have rather commonplace settings with real people, half of whom are known to the dreamer. In general, dreams are more unpleasant than pleasant, and they contain more aggression than friendly interaction and more misfortune than good fortune. Fear and anxiety, often quite intense, are common REM dreams (Hobson, 1996). Some dreams are in "living color," while others are in black and white. . . .   (6)

   Some people are troubled by unpleasant recurring dreams. The two most common themes involve being chased or falling (Stark, 1984).

People who have recurring dreams seem to have more minor physical complaints, greater stress, and more anxiety and depression than other people (Brown & Donderi, 1986). Is there anything that can be done to stop recurring dreams? Some people have been taught to use lucid dreaming to bring about satisfactory resolutions to their unpleasant recurring dreams. (7)

Have you ever experienced a **lucid dream**—one during which you were aware that you were dreaming? If so, you are among the 10% who claim to have this ability. Many lucid dreamers are able to change a dream while it is in progress, and a few virtuosos claim to be able to dream about any subject at will (Gackenbach & Bosveld, 1989; La Berge, 1981). (8)

Interpreting Dreams: Are There Hidden Meanings in Dreams?

Sigmund Freud believed that dreams function to satisfy unconscious sexual and aggressive wishes. Because such wishes are unacceptable to the dreamer, they have to be disguised and therefore appear in a dream in symbolic form. Freud (1900/1953a) claimed that objects such as sticks, umbrellas, tree trunks and guns symbolize the male sex organ; objects such as chests, cupboards, and boxes represent the female sex organ. Freud differentiated between the *manifest content* of the dream—the dream as recalled by the dreamer—and the underlying meaning of the dream, called the *latent content*, which he considered more significant. (9)

In recent years there has been a major shift away from Freudian interpretation of dreams. Now, there is greater focus on the manifest content, the actual dream itself, rather than on searching for symbolic meanings that can be interpreted to reveal some underlying personal conflict. The symbols in dreams, when analyzed, are now perceived as being specific to the individual rather than as having standard or universal meanings for all dreamers. Furthermore, dreams are seen more as an expression of a broad range of the dreamer's concerns than as primarily an expression of sexual impulses (Webb, 1975). (10)

J. Allan Hobson (1988) rejects the notion that nature would equip humans with a capability and a need to dream dreams that would require a specialist to interpret. Hobson and McCarley (1977) advanced the *activation-synthesis hypothesis* of dreaming. This hypothesis suggests that dreams are simply the brain's attempt to make sense of random firing of brain cells during REM sleep. Just as people try to make sense of input from the environment during their waking hours, they try to find meaning in the conglomeration of sensations and memories that are generated internally by this random firing of brain cells. Hobson (1989) now believes that dreams also have psychological significance, because the meaning a person imposes reflects that person's experiences, remote memories, associations, drives, and fears.   (11)

The Function of REM Sleep: Necessary, but Why?

Other researchers suggest that REM sleep aids in information processing, helping people sift through daily experience, to organize and store in memory information that is relevant to them.   (12)

Animal studies provide strong evidence for a relationship between REM sleep and learning (Hennevin et al., 1995; Smith, 1995; Winson, 1990). Some studies have revealed that animals increase their REM sleep following learning sessions. Other studies have indicated that when animals are deprived of REM sleep after new learning, their performance on the learned task is impaired the following day. But depriving subjects of NREM sleep had no such effect in the studies.   (13)

Research has shown that REM sleep serves an information-processing function in humans and is involved in the consolidation of memories after human learning. Karni and others (1994) found that research participants learning a new perceptual skill showed an improvement in performance, with no additional practice, 8 to 10 hours later if they had a normal night's sleep or if the researchers disturbed only their NREM sleep. Performance did not improve, however, in those who were deprived of REM sleep.   (14)

An opposite view is proposed by Francis Crick and Graeme Mitchison (1983, 1995). They suggest that REM sleep functions as mental housecleaning, erasing trivial and unnecessary memories and clearing overloaded neural circuits that might interfere with memory and rational thinking. In other words, they say, people dream in order to forget.   (15)

There is no doubt that REM sleep serves an important function, even if psychologists do not know precisely what that function is. The fact that newborns have such a high percentage of REM sleep has led to the conclusion that REM sleep is necessary for maturation of the brain in infants (Marks et al., 1995). Furthermore, when people are deprived of REM sleep as a result of general sleep loss or illness, they will make up for the loss by getting an increased amount of REM sleep after the deprivation. This increase in the percentage of REM sleep to make up for REM deprivation is called a **REM rebound.** Because the intensity of REM sleep is increased during a REM rebound, nightmares can often occur. Alcohol, amphetamines, cocaine, and LSD suppress REM sleep, and withdrawal from these drugs results in a REM rebound (Porte & Hobson, 1996).   (16)

References

Brown, R. J., & Donderi, D. C. (1986). Dream content and self-reported well-being among recurrent dreamers, past-recurrent dreamers, and nonrecurrent dreamers. *Journal of Personality and Social Psychology, 50,* 612–623. [4]

Cipolli, C., Bolzani, R., Cornoldi, C., De Beni, R., & Fagioli, I. (1993). Bizarreness effect in dream recall. *Sleep,* 16, 163–170.

Crick, F., & Mitchison, G. (1983). The function of dream sleep. *Nature,* 304, 408–416.

Crick, F., & Mitchison, G. (1995). REM sleep and neural nets. *Behavioral Brain Research,* 69, 147–155.

Foulkes, D. (1996). Sleep and dreams: Dream research: 1952–1993. *Sleep,* 19, 609–624.

Freud, S. (1953a). The interpretation of dreams. In J. Strachey (Ed. and Trans.), *The standard edition of the complete psychological works of Sigmund Freud* (Vols. 4 and 5). London: Hogarth Press. (Original work published 1900). [4, 13]

Gackenbach, J., & Bosveld, J. (1989, October). Take control of your dreams. *Psychology Today,* pp. 27–32.

Griffith, R. M., Miyago, O., & Tago, A. (1958). The universality of typical dreams; Japanese vs. Americans. *American Anthropologist,* 60, 1173–1179.

Hall, C. S., and Van de Castle, R. L. (1966). *The content analysis of dreams.* New York: Appleton-Century-Crofts.

Hennevin, E., Hars, B., Maho, C., & Bloch V. (1995). Processing of learned information in paradoxical sleep; Relevance for memory. *Behaviorial Brain Research*, 69, 125–135.

Hobson, J. A. (1988). *The dreaming brain*. New York: Basic Books.

Hobson, J. A. (1989). *Sleep*. New York: Scientific American Library.

Hobson, J. A. (1996, February). How the brain goes out of its mind. *Harvard Mental Health Letter*, 12(8), 3–5.

Hobson, J. A., & McCarely, R. W. (1977). The brain as a dream state generator: An activation-synthesis hypothesis of the dream process. *American Journal of Psychiatry*, 134, 1335–1348.

Hobson, J. A. & Stickgold, R. (1995). The conscious state paradigm: A neurological approach to waking, sleeping, and dreaming. In M.S. Gazzaniga (Ed.), *The cognitive neurosciences*. Cambridge, MA: MIT Press.

Karni, A., Tanne, D., Rubenstein, B.S., Askenasy, J. J. M., & Sagi, D. (1994). Dependence on REM sleep of overnight improvement of a perceptual skill. *Science*, 265, 679–682.

Kleitman, N. (1960). Patterns of dreaming. *Scientific American,* 203, 82–88.

La Berge, S. P. (1981, January). Lucid dreaming: Directing the action as it happens. *Psychology Today*, pp. 48–57.

Marks, I. M. (1995). Advances in behavioral-cognitive therapy of social phobia. *Journal of Clinical Psychiatry*, 56 (5, Suppl.), 25–31.

Porte, H. S., and Hobson, J. A. (1996). Physical motion in dreams: One measure of three theories. *Sleep*, 105, 3329–3335.

Smith, C. (1995). Sleep states and memory processes. *Behavioural Brain Research*, 69, 137–145.

Snyder, F. (1971). Psychophysiology of human sleep. *Clinical Neurosurgery*, 18, 503–536.

Stark, E. (1984, October). Answer this question: Responses: To sleep, perchance to dream. *Psychology Today*, p. 16.

Webb, W. B. (1975). *Sleep: The gentle tyrant*. Englewood Cliffs, NJ: Prentice-Hall.

Winson, J. (1990). The meaning of dreams. *Scientific American*, 263, 86–96.

EXPLORING VOCABULARY

Look up the terms REM sleep and NREM sleep. How does knowing these definitions enhance your understanding of the excerpt? Where did you find these definitions?

PROFILING EVENTS

Using the profile sheet on page 114, write a profile of dreaming. You may have to read between the lines—or make inferences—to address some of the categories. When you are finished, discuss your answers with a small group of your peers or with the entire class.

EXPLORING THE TEXT

1. What do the parentheses enclosing names and dates mean? What does it mean when there is more than one name and/or date with the parentheses?
2. How might this piece be different if it were an essay instead of a textbook excerpt? What features might be added? What features might be deleted?
3. Why do the authors put some words or phrases in bold and others in italics? What does each signify?
4. How do the headings help the reader?

EXPLORING IDEAS

1. After reading this piece, what do you think the dream you wrote about actually means? (Review your annotations.)
2. Which theory about the meaning of dreams do you find more compelling? Why?
3. If you were studying this piece for a test in a psychology class, what information would you expect to find on the test? Why?
4. Why is REM sleep important? Do you get enough REM sleep?

Last Flight (LETTER)

ISAO MATSUO

PREREADING

Look up the word *kamikaze* in a dictionary and an encyclopedia. Make some notes about what you learn and share your research with your classmates.

ANNOTATING

While reading, underline any words, phrases, or sentences that surprise or shock you. In the margins, explain why you are surprised or shocked.

28 October 1944

Dear Parents,

Please congratulate me. I have been given a splendid opportunity to die. This is my last day. The destiny of our homeland hinges on the decisive battle in the seas to the south where I shall fall like a blossom from a radiant cherry tree.   (1)

I shall be a shield for His Majesty and die cleanly along with my squadron leader and other friends. I wish that I could be born seven times, each time to smite the enemy.   (2)

How I appreciate this chance to die like a man! I am grateful from the depths of my heart to the parents who have reared me with their constant prayer and tender love. And I am grateful as well to my squadron leader and superior officers who have looked after me as if I were their own son and given me such careful training.   (3)

Thank you, my parents, for the 23 years during which you have cared for me and inspired me. I hope that my present deed will in some small way repay what you have done for me. Think well of me and know that your Isao died for our country. This is my last wish, and there is nothing else that I desire.

(4)

I shall return in spirit and look forward to your visit at the Yasukuni Shrine. Please take good care of yourselves.

(5)

How glorious is the Special Attack Corps' Giretsu Unit whose Suisei bombers will attack the enemy. Movie cameramen have been here to take our pictures. It is possible that you may see us in newsreels at the theater.

(6)

We are 16 warriors manning the bombers. May our death be as sudden and clean as the shattering of crystal.

(7)

Written at Manila on the eve of our sortie.

(8)

Isao

EXPLORING VOCABULARY

List the words from the reading that you do not understand and try to figure out their meanings by using context clues (see page 200). Then look the words up in a dictionary to see how closely your definitions match those in the dictionary.

PROFILING EVENTS

Using the profile sheet on page 114, write a profile of Isao's last flight. You may have to read between the lines—or make inferences—to address some of the categories. When you are finished, discuss your answers with a small group of your peers or with the entire class.

EXPLORING THE TEXT

1. What is the tone of this letter? How do you know?
2. Does Matsuo's letter sound sincere?
3. Is Matsuo's purpose to inform his parents of his mission or to convince his parents that his mission is an honor?
4. What about this letter surprised or shocked you? (Review your annotations.)

EXPLORING IDEAS

1. Is it right for a country to ask one of its citizens to die while in service to that country?
2. Have you ever made a sacrifice for anyone? Why did you do it? Has anyone ever made a sacrifice for you?
3. How do you think Matsuo's parents felt when they received his letter?
4. If you knew you were going to die while serving your country, what would you write in a letter to your parents?

Because I could not stop for Death (POEM)

EMILY DICKINSON

PREREADING

Research the life of Emily Dickinson on the internet or in the library; then share your findings with your classmates.

ANNOTATING

While reading, underline any words you cannot readily define. In the margins, write a possible definition.

Because I could not stop for Death—
He kindly stopped for me—
The Carriage held but just Ourselves—
And Immortality.

We slowly drove—He knew no haste   (5)
And I had put away
My labor and my leisure too,
For His Civility—
We passed the School, where Children strove
At Recess—in the Ring—   (10)
We passed the Fields of Gazing Grain—
We passed the Setting Sun—

Or rather—He passed us—
The Dews drew quivering and chill—
For only Gossamer, my Gown—   (15)
My Tippet—only Tulle—

We paused before a House that seemed
A Swelling of the Ground—
The Roof was scarcely visible—
The Cornice—in the Ground—   (20)

Since then—'tis Centuries—and yet
Feels shorter than the Day
I first surmised the Horses' Heads
Were toward Eternity.

EXPLORING VOCABULARY

Look up the words you underlined while reading this essay and then check your definitions with those you found in the dictionary.

PROFILING EVENTS

Using the profile sheet on page 114, write a profile of the event described in the poem. You may have to read between the lines—or make inferences—to address some of the categories. When you are finished, discuss your answers with a small group of your peers or with the entire class.

EXPLORING THE TEXT

1. Why does Dickinson use so many dashes in her poem? (You may want to look up the function of a dash in a grammar handbook.)
2. Why does Dickinson capitalize the words that she does?
3. What is the speaker's tone?
4. Is the speaker a man or a woman? How do you know?

EXPLORING IDEAS

1. How did you feel while you were reading this poem? Can you relate to the speaker in any way?
2. What does the speaker seem to imply about life after death?
3. Do you believe in any sort of life after death? If so, what do you imagine it to be like?

Body Ritual among the Nacirema (ESSAY)

HORACE MINER

PREREADING

Look up the word *ritual* in the dictionary. When you feel you have an understanding of the word, describe in a free write a ritual that you perform everyday, every week, every month, or every year. Share your description with the class.

ANNOTATING

While reading, underline any rituals, activities, or beliefs described in the essay that you find shocking or bizarre. In the margins, note the reason you feel the way you do.

The anthropologist has become so familiar with the diversity of ways in which different people behave in similar situations that he is not apt to be surprised by even the most exotic customs. In fact, if all of the logically possible combinations of behavior had not been found somewhere in the world, he is apt to suspect that they must be present in some yet undescribed tribe. This point has, in fact, been expressed with respect to clan organization by Murdock (1949:71). In this light, the magical beliefs and practices of the Nacirema present such unusual aspects that it seems desirable to describe them as an example of the extremes to which human behavior can go.   (1)

Professor Linton first brought the ritual among the Nacirema to the attention of anthropologists twenty years ago (1936: 326), but the culture of this people is still very poorly understood. They are a North American group living in the territory between the Canadian Cree, the Yaqui and Tarahumare of Mexico, and the Carib and Arawak of the Antilles. Little is known of their origin, although tradition states that they came from the east. According to Nacirema mythology, their nation was originated by a culture hero, Notgnihsaw, who is otherwise known for two great feats of strength—the throwing of a piece of wampum across the river Pa-To-Mac and the chopping down of a cherry tree in which the Spirit of Truth resided. (2)

Nacirema culture is characterized by a highly developed market economy which has evolved in a rich natural habitat. While much of the people's time is devoted to economic pursuits, a large part of the fruits of these labors and a considerable portion of the day are spent in ritual activity. The focus of this activity is the human body, the appearance and health of which loom as a dominant concern in the ethos of the people. While such a concern is certainly not unusual, its ceremonial aspects and associated philosophy are unique. (3)

The fundamental belief underlying the whole system appears to be that the human body is ugly and that its natural tendency is to debility and disease. Incarcerated in such a body, man's only hope is to avert these characteristics through the use of the powerful influences of ritual and ceremony. Every household has one or more shrines devoted to this purpose. The more powerful individuals in the society have several shrines in their houses and, in fact, the opulence of a house is often referred to in terms of the number of such ritual centers it possesses. Most houses are of wattle and daub construction, but the shrine rooms of the more wealthy are walled with stone. Poorer families imitate the rich by applying pottery plaques to their shrine walls. (4)

While each family has at least one such shrine, the rituals associated with it are not family ceremonies but are private and secret. The rites are normally only discussed with children, and then only during the period when they are being initiated into these mysteries. I was able, however, to establish sufficient rapport with the natives to examine these shrines and to have the rituals described to me. (5)

The focal point of the shrine is a box or chest which is built into the wall. In this chest are kept the many charms and magical potions without which no native believes he could live. These preparations are secured from a variety of specialized practitioners. The most powerful of these are the medicine men, whose assistance must be rewarded with substantial gifts. However, the medicine men do not provide the curative potions for their clients, but decide what the ingredients should be and then write them down in an ancient and secret language. This writing is understood only by the medicine men and by the herbalists who, for another gift, provide the required charm. (6)

The charm is not disposed of after it has served its purpose, but is placed in the charm-box of the household shrine. As these magical materials are specific for certain ills, and the real or imagined maladies of the people are many, the charm-box is usually full to overflowing. The magical packets are so numerous that people forget what their purposes were and fear to use them again. While the natives are very vague about this point, we can only assume that the idea in retaining all the old magical materials is that their presence in the charm-box, before which the body rituals are conducted, will in some way protect the worshipper. (7)

Beneath the charm-box is a small font. Each day every member of the family, in succession, enters the shrine room, bows his head before the charm-box, mingles different sorts of holy water in the font, and proceeds with a brief rite of ablution. The holy waters are secured from the Water Temple of the community, where the priests conduct elaborate ceremonies to make the liquid ritually pure. (8)

In the hierarchy of magical practitioners, and below the medicine men in prestige, are specialists whose designation is best translated "holy-mouth-men." The Nacirema have an almost pathological horror of and fascination with the mouth, the condition of which is believed to have a supernatural influence on all social relationships. Were it not for the rituals of the mouth, they believe that their teeth would fall out, their gums bleed, their jaws shrink, their friends desert them, and their lovers reject them. They also believe that a strong relationship exists between oral and moral characteristics. For example, there is a ritual ablution of the mouth for children which is supposed to improve their moral fiber. (9)

The daily body ritual performed by everyone includes a mouth-rite. Despite the fact that these people are so punctilious about the care of the mouth, this rite involves a practice which strikes the uninitiated stranger as revolting. It was reported to me that the ritual consists of inserting a small bundle of hog hairs into the mouth, along with certain magical powders, and then moving the bundle in a highly formalized series of gestures. (10)

In addition to the private mouth-rite, the people seek out a holy-mouth-man once or twice a year. These practitioners have an impressive set of paraphernalia, consisting of a variety of augers, awls, probes, and prods. The use of these objects in the exorcism of the evils of the mouth involves almost unbelievable ritual torture of the client. The holy-mouth-man opens the client's mouth and, using the above mentioned tools, enlarges any holes which decay may have created in the teeth. Magical materials are put into these holes. If there are no naturally occurring holes in the teeth, large sections of one or more teeth are gouged out so that the supernatural substances can be applied. In the client's view, the purpose of these ministrations is to arrest decay and to draw friends. The extremely sacred and traditional character of the rite is evident in the fact that the natives return to the holy-mouth-men year after year, despite the fact that their teeth continue to decay.   (11)

It is to be hoped that, when a thorough study of the Nacirema is made, there will be careful inquiry into the personality structure of these people. One has but to watch the gleam in the eye of a holy-mouth-man, as he jabs an awl into an exposed nerve, to suspect that a certain amount of sadism is involved. If this can be established, a very interesting pattern emerges, for most of the population shows definite masochistic tendencies. It was to these that Professor Linton referred in discussing a distinctive part of the daily body ritual which is performed only by men. This part of the rite involves scraping and lacerating the surface of the face with a sharp instrument. Special woman's rites are performed only four times during each lunar month, but what they lack in frequency is made up in barbarity. As part of this ceremony, women bake their heads in small ovens for about an hour. The theoretically interesting point is that what seems to be a preponderantly masochistic people have developed sadistic specialists. . . .   (12)

In conclusion, mention must be made of certain practices which have their base in native esthetics but which depend upon the pervasive aversion to the natural body and its functions. There are ritual fasts to make fat people thin and ceremonial feasts to make thin people fat. Still other rites are used to make women's breasts larger if they are small, and smaller if they are large. General dissatisfaction with breast shape is symbolized in the fact that the ideal form is virtually outside the range of human variation. A few women afflicted with almost inhuman hypermammary development are so idolized that they make a handsome living by simply going from village to village and permitting the natives to stare at them for a fee.   (13)

Reference has already been made to the fact that excretory functions are ritualized, routinized, and relegated to secrecy. Natural reproductive functions are similarly distorted. Intercourse is a taboo topic and scheduled as an act. Efforts are made to avoid pregnancy by the use of magical materials or by limiting intercourse to certain phases of the moon. Conception is actually very infrequent. When pregnant, women dress so as to hide their condition. Parturition takes place in secret, without friends or relatives to assist, and the majority of women do not nurse their infants.   (14)

Our view of the ritual life of the Nacirema has certainly shown them to be a magic-ridden people. It is hard to understand how they have managed to exist so long under the burdens which they have imposed on themselves. But even such exotic customs as these take on real meaning when they are viewed with the insight provided by Malinowski when he wrote (1949:70):

> *Looking from far and above, from our high places of safety in the developed civilization, it is easy to see all the crudity and irrelevance of magic. But without its power and guidance early man could not have mastered his practical difficulties as he has done, nor could man have advanced to the higher stages of civilization.*   (15)

References

Linton, Ralph. 1936. *The Study of Man.* New York: D Appleton-Century Co.

Malinowski, Bronislaw. 1948. *Magic, Science, and Religion.* Glenco: The Free Press.

Murdock, George P. 1949. *Social Structure.* New York: The Macmillan Co.

EXPLORING VOCABULARY

Using the lists of word parts on page 203, try to define the following words: anthropologist (paragraph 1), philosophy (paragraph 3), pathological (paragraph 9), hypermammary (paragraph 13), reproductive (paragraph 14), and infrequent (paragraph 14).

PROFILING EVENTS

Using the profile sheet on page 114, write a profile of one of the rituals of the Nacirema. You may have to read between the lines—or make inferences—to address some of the categories. When you are finished, discuss your answers with a small group of your peers or with the entire class.

EXPLORING TEXT

1. Who are the Nacirema? What distinct clues does the author give us to their real identity?
2. Why does the author choose to write about the Nacirema in this manner?
3. What is the main idea of this excerpt?
4. For what audience is the author writing?

EXPLORING IDEAS

1. In paragraph two, Miner writes, ". . . the culture of this people is still very poorly understood." Do you agree with this or disagree with this? Why?
2. Which ritual that Miner describes shocks you the most? Why? (Review your annotations.)
3. Do you agree or disagree with Miner's assertion in paragraph four that the Nacirema believe "the human body is ugly and that its natural tendency is to debility and disease"? Why?
4. Read the last paragraph several times. What does it mean? What is the author trying to say about the Nacirema and other modern cultures without saying it directly?

38 Who Saw Murder Didn't Call Police (ESSAY)

MARTIN GANSBERG

PREREADING

Free write about a time you witnessed a crime. What happened and how did you respond? If you have never witnessed a crime, create a scenario and speculate as to how you might act.

ANNOTATING

While reading, underline the words, phrases, or sentences the author uses to describe the people who witnessed the murder. In the margins, write one adjective to describe the person(s).

For more than half an hour 38 respectable, law-abiding citizens in Queens watched a killer stalk and stab a woman in three separate attacks in Kew Gardens. (1)

Twice their chatter and the sudden glow of their bedroom lights interrupted him and frightened him off. Each time he returned, sought her out, and stabbed her again. Not one person telephoned the police during the assault; one witness called after the woman was dead. (2)

That was two weeks ago today. (3)

Still shocked is Assistant Chief Inspector Frederick M. Lussen, in charge of the borough's detectives and a veteran of 25 years of homicide investigations. He can give a matter-of-fact recitation on many murders. But the Kew Gardens slaying baffles him—not because it is a murder, but because the "good people" failed to call the police. (4)

"As we have reconstructed the crime," he said, "the assailant had three chances to kill this woman during a 35-minute period. He

returned twice to complete the job. If we had been called when he
first attacked, the woman might not be dead now." (5)

This is what the police say happened beginning at 3:20 a.m. in the
staid, middle-class, tree-lined Austin Street area: (6)

Twenty-eight-year-old Catherine Genovese, who was called Kitty
by almost everyone in the neighborhood, was returning home from
her job as manager of a bar in Hollis. She parked her red Fiat in a lot
adjacent to the Kew Gardens Long Island Rail Road Station, facing
Mowbray Place. Like many residents of the neighborhood, she had
parked there day after day since her arrival from Connecticut a year
ago, although the railroad frowns on the practice. (7)

She turned off the lights of her car, locked the door, and started to
walk the 100 feet to the entrance of her apartment at 82-70 Austin
Street, which is in a Tudor building, with stores in the first floor and
apartments on the second. (8)

The entrance to the apartment is in the rear of the building because
the front is rented to retail stores. At night the quiet neighborhood is
shrouded in the slumbering darkness that marks most residential areas. (9)

Miss Genovese noticed a man at the far end of the lot, near a seven-
story apartment house at 82-40 Austin Street. She halted. Then, nervously,
she headed up Austin Street toward Lefferts Boulevard, where there is a
call box to the 102nd Police Precinct in nearby Richmond Hill. (10)

She got as far as the street light in front of a bookstore before the
man grabbed her. She screamed. Lights went on in the 10-story
apartment house at 82-67 Austin Street, which faces the bookstore.
Windows slid open and voices punctuated the early-morning stillness. (11)

Miss Genovese screamed: "Oh, my God, he stabbed me! Please help
me! Please help me!" (12)

From one of the upper windows in the apartment house, a man
called down: "Let that girl alone!" (13)

The assailant looked up at him, shrugged, and walked down Austin
Street toward a white sedan parked a short distance away. Miss
Genovese struggled to her feet. (14)

Lights went out. The killer returned to Miss Genovese, now trying
to make her way around the side of the building by the parking lot to
get to her apartment. The assailant stabbed her again. (15)

"I'm dying!" she shrieked. "I'm dying!"   (16)

Windows were opened again, and lights went on in many apartments. The assailant got into his car and drove away. Miss Genovese staggered to her feet. A city bus, O-10, the Lefferts Boulevard line to Kennedy International Airport, passed. It was 3:35 A.M.   (17)

The assailant returned. By then, Miss Genovese had crawled to the back of the building, where the freshly painted brown doors to the apartment house held out hope for safety. The killer tried the first door; she wasn't there. At the second door, 82-62 Austin Street, he saw her slumped on the floor at the foot of the stairs. He stabbed her a third time—fatally.   (18)

It was 3:50 by the time the police received their first call, from a man who was a neighbor of Miss Genovese. In two minutes they were at the scene. The neighbor, a 70-year-old woman, and another woman were the only persons on the street. Nobody else came forward.   (19)

The man explained that he had called the police after much deliberation. He had phoned a friend in Nassau County for advice and then he had crossed the roof of the building to the apartment of the elderly woman to get her to make a call.   (20)

"I didn't want to get involved," he sheepishly told the police.   (21)

Six days later, the police arrested Winston Moseley, a 29-year-old business machine operator, and charged him with homicide. Moseley had no previous record. He is married, has two children and owns a home at 133-19 Sutter Avenue, South Ozone Park, Queens. On Wednesday, a court committed him to Kings County Hospital for psychiatric observation.   (22)

When questioned by the police, Moseley also said that he had slain Mrs. Annie May Johnson, 24, of 146-12 133rd Avenue, Jamaica, on Feb. 29 and Barbara Kralik, 15, of 174-17 140th Avenue, Springfield Gardens, last July. In the Kralik case, the police are holding Alvin L. Mitchell, who is said to have confessed to that slaying.   (23)

The police stressed how simple it would have been to have gotten in touch with them. "A phone call," said one of the detectives, "would have done it." The police may be reached by dialing "O" for operator or Spring 7-3100.   (24)

Today witnesses from the neighborhood, which is made up of one-family homes in the $35,000 to $60,000 range with the exception of the two apartment houses near the railroad station, find it difficult to explain why they didn't call the police.   (25)

A housewife, knowingly, if quite casually, said, "We thought it was a lovers' quarrel." A husband and wife both said, "Frankly, we were afraid." They seemed aware of the fact that events might have been different. A distraught woman wiping her hands in her apron, said, "I didn't want my husband to get involved."   (26)

One couple, now willing to talk about that night, said they heard the first screams. The husband looked thoughtfully at the bookstore where the killer first grabbed Miss Genovese.   (27)

"We went to the window to see what was happening," he said, "but the light from our bedroom made it difficult to see the street." The wife, still apprehensive, added: "I put out the light and we were able to see better."   (28)

Asked why they hadn't called the police, she shrugged and replied: "I don't know."   (29)

A man peeked out from a slight opening in the doorway to his apartment and rattled off an account of the killer's second attack. Why hadn't he called the police at the time? "I was tired," he said without emotion. "I went back to bed."   (30)

It was 4:25 A.M. when the ambulance arrived to take the body of Miss Genovese. It drove off. "Then," a solemn police detective said, "the people came out."   (31)

EXPLORING VOCABULARY

Review your annotations and list the adjectives you used to describe the thirty-eight people. Share your adjectives with the class.

PROFILING EVENTS

Using the profile sheet on page 114, write a profile of the murder of Kitty Genovese. You may have to read between the lines—or make inferences—to address some of the categories. When you are finished, discuss your answers with a small group of your peers or with the entire class.

EXPLORING THE TEXT

1. What is the author's purpose?

2. What is the author's tone?
3. For what type of audience is this author writing?
4. Does this article have a main idea? If so, what is it?

EXPLORING IDEAS

1. What have you been taught about helping others? Did the thirty-eight people in this article live up to what you have been taught?
2. What would you do if you were in the same position as the thirty-eight people?
3. Do you think these people should be charged as accessories to the crime? Why or why not?
4. This article was written in 1964. Do you think people are more responsive to crime now or less responsive? Why?

Growing Up Game (ESSAY)

BRENDA PETERSON

PREREADING

Do some reading about the food chain. Try to discover what the food chain is and where humans are on the food chain. Share your findings with the class.

ANNOTATING

While reading, underline any words, phrases, or sentences that express the author's opinion, belief, or commentary. In the margins, note whether you agree or disagree with the author.

When I went off to college my father gave me, as part of my tuition, 50 pounds of moose meat. In 1969, eating moose meat at the University of California was a contradiction in terms. Hippies didn't hunt. I lived in a rambling Victorian house which boasted sweeping circular staircases, built-in lofts, and a landlady who dreamed of opening her own health food restaurant. I told my housemates that my moose meat in its nondescript white butcher paper was from a side of beef my father had bought. The carnivores in the house helped me finish off such suppers as sweet and sour mooseballs, mooseburgers (garnished with the obligatory avocado and sprouts), and mooseghetti. The same dinner guests who remarked upon the lean sweetness of the meat would have recoiled if I'd told them the not-so-simple truth: that I grew up on game, and the moose they were eating had been brought down, with one shot through his magnificent heart, by my father—a man who had hunted all his life and all of mine. (1)

One of my earliest memories is of crawling across the vast continent of crinkled linoleum in our Forest Service cabin kitchen, down splintered back steps, through wildflowers growing wheat-high. I was eye-level with grasshoppers who scolded me on my first solo trip outside. I made it to the shed, a cool and comfortingly square shelter that held phantasmagoric metal parts; they smelled good, like dirt and grease. I had played a long time in this shed before some maternal shriek made me lift up on my haunches to listen to those urgent, possessive sounds that were my name. Rearing up, my head bumped into something hanging in the dark; gleaming white, it felt sleek and cold against my cheek. Its smell was dense and musty and not unlike the slabs of my grandmother's great arms after her cool, evening sponge baths. In that shed I looked up and saw the flensed body of a doe; it swung gently, slapping my face. I felt then as I do even now when eating game: horror and awe and hunger.   (2)

Growing up those first years on a forest station high in the Sierra was somewhat like belonging to a white tribe. The men hiked off every day into their forest and the women stayed behind in the circle of official cabins, breeding. So far away from a store, we ate venison and squirrel, rattlesnake and duck. My brother's first rattle, in fact, was from a King Rattler my father killed as we watched, by snatching it up with a stick and winding it, whip-like, around a redwood sapling. Rattlesnake tastes just like chicken, but has many fragile bones to slither one's way through; we also ate salmon, rabbit, and geese galore. The game was accompanied by such daily garden dainties as fried okra, mustard greens, corn fritters, wilted lettuce (our favorite because of the rare blackened bacon), new potatoes and peas, stewed tomatoes, barbecued butter beans.   (3)

I was 4 before I ever had a beef hamburger and I remember being disappointed by its fatty, nothing taste and the way it fell apart at the seams whenever my teeth sank into it. Smoked pork shoulder came much later in the South; and I was 21, living in New York City, before I ever tasted leg of lamb. I approached that glazed rack of meat with a certain guilty self-consciousness, as if I unfairly stalked those sweet-tempered white creatures myself. But how would I explain my squeamishness to those urban sophisticates? How explain that I was shy with mutton when I had been bred on wild things?   (4)

Part of it, I suspect, had to do with the belief I'd also been bred on—we become the spirit and body of the animals we eat. As a child eating venison I liked to think of myself as lean and lovely just like the deer. I would never be caught dead just grazing while some man who wasn't even a skillful hunter crept up and konked me over the head. If someone wanted to hunt me, he must be wily and outwitting. He must earn me.   (5)

My father also taught us as children that animals were our brothers and sisters under their skin. They died so that we might live. And of this sacrifice we must be mindful. "God make us grateful for what we are about to receive" took on a new meaning when one knew the animal's struggle pitted against our own appetite. We also used *all* the animal so that an elk became elk steaks, stew, salami, and sausage. His head and horns went on the wall to watch us more earnestly than any babysitter, and every Christmas Eve we had a ceremony of making our own Moccasins for the new year out of whatever Father had tanned. "Nothing wasted," my father would always say, or, as we munched on sausage cookies made from moosemeat or venison, "Think about who you're eating." We thought of ourselves as intricately linked to the food chain. We knew, for example, that a forest fire meant, at the end of the line, we'd suffer too. We'd have buck stew instead of venison steak and the meat would be stringy, withered-tasting because in the animal kingdom, as it seemed with humans, only the meanest and leanest and orneriest survived.   (6)

Once when I was in my early teens, I went along on a hunting trip as the "main cook and bottle-washer," though I don't remember any bottles; none of these hunters drank alcohol. There was something else coursing through their veins as they rose long before dawn and disappeared, returning to my little camp most often dragging a doe or pheasant or rabbit. We ate innumerable cornmeal-fried catfish, had rabbit stew seasoned only with blood and black pepper.   (7)

This hunting trip was the first time I remember eating game as a conscious act. My father and Buddy Earl shot a big doe and she lay with me in the back of the tarp-draped station wagon all the way home. It was not the smell I minded; it was the glazed great, dark eyes and the way the head flopped around crazily on what I knew was once a graceful neck. I found myself petting this doe, murmuring all those graces we'd been taught so long ago as children: *Thank you for the sacrifice, thank you for letting us be like you so that we can grow up strong as game.* But there was an uneasiness in me that night as I bounced along in the back of the car with the deer.   (8)

What was uneasy is still uneasy—perhaps it always will be. It's not easy when one really starts thinking about all this: the eating game, the food chain, the sacrifice of one for the other. It's never easy when one begins to think about one's most basic actions, like eating. Like becoming what one eats: lean and lovely and mortal.   (9)

Why should it be that the purchase of meat at a butcher shop is somehow more righteous than eating something wild? Perhaps it has to do with our collective unconscious that sees the animal bred for slaughter as doomed. But that wild doe or moose might make it without the hunter. Perhaps on this primitive level of archetype and unconscious knowing we even believe that what's wild lives forever.   (10)

My father once told this story around a hunting campfire. His own father, who raised cattle during the Depression on a dirt farm in the Ozarks, once fell on such hard times that he had to butcher the pet lamb for supper. My father, bred on game or their own hogs all his life, took one look at the family pet on that meat platter and pushed his plate away from him. His siblings followed suit. To hear my grandfather tell it, it was the funniest thing he'd ever seen. "They just couldn't eat Bo-Peep," Grandfather said. And to hear my father tell it years later around the campfire, it was funny, but I saw for the first time his sadness. And I realized that eating had become a conscious act for him that day at the dinner table when Bo-Peep offered herself up.   (11)

Now when someone offers me game I will eat it with all the qualms and memories and reverence with which I grew up eating it. And I think it will always be this feeling of horror and awe and hunger. And something else—full knowledge of what I do, what I become.   (12)

EXPLORING VOCABULARY

Look up the word *conscious* in the dictionary and figure out which definition applies to the way Peterson uses the word in paragraph eight.

PROFILING EVENTS

Using the profile sheet on page 114, write a profile of eating from Peterson's point of view. You may have to read between the lines—or make inferences—to address some of the categories. When you are finished, discuss your answers with a small group of your peers or with the entire class.

EXPLORING THE TEXT

1. How many specific memories does the author share? Which memories are most effective?
2. What is the main idea? (Review your annotations for clues.)
3. Does Peterson use topic sentences in every body paragraph?
4. What transitional devices does Peterson use?

EXPLORING IDEAS

1. How involved are you in the preparation of your own meals?
2. Have you ever eaten wild game? When? What did it taste like?
3. In paragraph ten, Peterson asks, "Why should it be that the purchase of meat at a butcher shop is somehow more righteous than eating something wild?" How would you answer this question?
4. Do you eat consciously? What actions do you engage in consciously?

The Story of an Hour (SHORT STORY)

KATE CHOPIN

PREREADING

Free write about a time when you were simultaneously happy and sad or about a person whom you loved and didn't love at the same time. Share your free write with the class.

ANNOTATING

While reading, underline any words, phrases, or sentences that tell you how Louise, the main character, feels about her husband. In the margins, note the emotion she is experiencing.

Knowing that Mrs. Mallard was afflicted with a heart trouble, great care was taken to break to her as gently as possible the news of her husband's death. (1)

It was her sister Josephine who told her, in broken sentences, veiled hints that revealed in half concealing. Her husband's friend Richards was there, too near her. It was he who had been in the newspaper office when intelligence of the railroad disaster was received, with Brently Mallard's name leading the list of "killed." He had taken the time to assure himself of its truth by a second telegram, and had hastened to forestall any less careful, less tender friend in bearing the sad message. (2)

She did not hear the story as many women have heard the same, with a paralyzed inability to accept its significance. She wept at once, with sudden, wild abandonment, in her sister's arms. When the storm of grief had spent itself she went away to her room alone. She would have no one follow her. (3)

There stood, facing the open window, a comfortable, roomy armchair. Into this she sank, pressed down by a physical exhaustion that haunted her body and seemed to reach down into her soul. (4)

She could see in the open square before her house the tops of the trees that were all aquiver with the new spring life. The delicious breath of rain was in the air. In the street below a peddler was crying his wares. The notes of the distant song which some one was singing reached her faintly, and countless sparrows were twittering in the eaves. (5)

There were patches of blue sky showing here and there through the clouds that had met and piled above the other in the west facing her window. (6)

She sat with her head thrown back upon the cushion of the chair quite motionless, except when a sob came up into her throat and shook her, as a child who has cried itself to sleep continues to sob in its dreams. (7)

She was young, with a fair, calm face, whose lines bespoke repression and even a certain strength. But now there was a dull stare in her eyes, whose gaze was fixed away off yonder on one of those patches of blue in the sky. It was not a glance of reflection, but rather indicated a suspension of intelligent thought. (8)

There was something coming to her and she was waiting for it fearfully. What was it? She did not know; it was too subtle and elusive to name. But she felt it, creeping out of the sky, reaching toward her through the sounds, the scents, the color that filled the air. (9)

Now her bosom rose and fell tumultuously. She was beginning to recognize this thing that was approaching to possess her, and she was striving to beat it back with her will—as powerless as her two white slender hands would have been. (10)

When she abandoned herself a little whispered word escaped her slightly parted lips. She said it over and over under her breath: "Free, free, free!" The vacant stare and the look of terror that had followed it went from her eyes. They stayed keen and bright. Her pulses beat fast, and the coursing blood warmed and relaxed every inch of her body. (11)

She did not stop to ask if it were not a monstrous joy that held her. A clear and exalted perception enabled her to dismiss the suggestion as trivial. (12)

She knew that she would weep again when she saw the kind, tender hands folded in death; the face that had never looked save with love upon her, fixed and gray and dead. But she saw beyond that bitter moment a long procession of years to come that would belong to her absolutely. And she opened and spread her arms out to them in welcome.   (13)

There would be no one to live for during those coming years; she would live for herself. There would be no powerful will bending her in that blind persistence with which men and women believe they have a right to impose a private will upon a fellow-creature. A kind intention or a cruel intention made the act seem no less a crime as she looked upon it in that brief moment of illumination.   (14)

And yet she had loved him—sometimes. Often she had not. What did it matter! What could love, the unsolved mystery, count for in the face of this possession of self-assertion which she suddenly recognized as the strongest impulse of her being!   (15)

"Free! Body and soul free!" she kept whispering.   (16)

Josephine was kneeling before the closed door with her lips to the keyhole, imploring for admission. "Louise, open the door! I beg; open the door—you will make yourself ill. What are you doing, Louise? For heaven's sake open the door."   (17)

"Go away. I am not making myself ill." No; she was drinking in a very elixir of life through that open window.   (18)

Her fancy was running riot along those days ahead of her. Spring days, and summer days, and all sorts of days that would be her own. She breathed a quick prayer that life might be long. It was only yesterday she had thought with a shudder that life might be long.   (19)

She arose at length and opened the door to her sister's importunities. There was a feverish triumph in her eyes, and she carried herself unwittingly like a goddess of Victory. She clasped her sister's waist, and together they descended the stairs. Richards stood waiting for them at the bottom.   (20)

Some one was opening the front door with a latchkey. It was Brently Mallard who entered, a little travel-stained, composedly carrying his grip-sack and umbrella. He had been far from the scene of the accident, and did not even know there had been one. He stood amazed at Josephine's piercing cry; at Richards' quick motion to screen him from the view of his wife.   (21)

But Richards was too late.   (22)

When the doctors came they said she had died of heart disease—of joy that kills.   (23)

EXPLORING VOCABULARY

Define the word *foreshadow*. After you feel you understand its meaning, read the story again with a small group of your classmates and identify where the author uses foreshadowing.

PROFILING EVENTS

Using the profile sheet on page 114, write a profile of the event leading up to Louise's death. You may have to read between the lines—or make inferences—to address some of the categories. When you are finished, discuss your answers with a small group of your peers or with the entire class.

EXPLORING THE TEXT

1. Why does Chopin call this work "The Story of an Hour"?
2. Who is narrating this story? What do we know about the narrator?
3. What is the theme?

EXPLORINGIDEAS

1. Describe Louise's feelings toward her husband. (Review your annotations.)
2. What is Louise's attitude toward marriage?
3. In paragraph twelve, the narrator tells us that Louise "did not stop to ask if it were not a monstrous joy that held her." What does this line mean?
4. In the last sentence of the story, we are told that Louise died "of joy that kills." What does this mean? Can it have two meanings at the same time?

SUGGESTIONS FOR READING BOOKS ABOUT EVENTS

Dead Man Walking by Sister Helen Prejean

The Perfect Storm by Sebastian Junger

A Gathering of Old Men by Ernest J. Gaines

SUGGESTIONS FOR SUMMARIZING ESSAYS ABOUT EVENTS

Choose one of the following works from Unit Three and write a summary. Follow the guidelines for writing a summary on page 207.

"Growing Up Game" by Brenda Peterson

"38 Who Saw Murder Didn't Call Police" by Martin Gansberg

SUGGESTIONS FOR WRITING ABOUT EVENTS

1. Choose an event in your life that made you see the world differently and write an essay about it. Show the reader what happened by using detail and dialogue; then tell the reader the significance of the event.

2. Choose an event that made you appreciate your family and write an essay about it.

3. Write an essay about a daily, weekly, monthly, or yearly ritual that you practice. Describe the ritual in detail and discuss its significance in your life.

4. Observe an event—a concert, a tattooing, a birthday party, a wedding, etc.—and write an essay in which you report what happened. Use the profile sheet in this unit to help you gather your information.

5. Read one of the books listed and write a profile of one of the events written about in the book. Use the profile sheet in this unit to help you gather your information.

6. Write a letter to the editor of your local newspaper in response to an event you read about in the paper.

7. Interview one of your classmates or friends about an event that he or she experienced. Then write an essay profiling that event. Use the profile sheet in this unit to help you gather information.

PROFILING EVENTS

Fill in the following information about one or more of the events you have read about in Unit Three. Remember that the information in some categories may not be directly stated; it may be implied. If it is implied, use clues given by the author to infer the answer. Remember also that the information in some categories may not be directly stated or implied, so do not just guess at any given category.

TYPE _____

CAUSE _____

PURPOSE/FUNCTION _____

LOCATION(S) _____

SEQUENCE _____

TIME LAPSED _____

PARTICIPANT(S) _____

NUMBER _____

NAME(S) _____

AGE(S) _____

SOCIOECONOMIC CLASS(ES) _____

EDUCATIONAL LEVEL(S) _____

CULTURAL/PHILOSOPHICAL AFFILIATION(S) _____

CONFLICT(S) INVOLVED _____

TRIUMPH(S) INVOLVED _____

CONSEQUENCES _____

SIGNIFICANCE _____

UNIT IV

PHENOMENA

Looking Up At Something   (POEM)

D<small>ENNIS</small> S<small>AMPSON</small>

PREREADING

Free write about a time you saw, experienced, or felt something very moving but were afraid other people wouldn't believe you.

ANNOTATING

While reading, place a slash (/) at the end of each sentence. Read the poem again, sentence by sentence, and note in the margins what each sentence means.

> One night, in Ohio,
>> hearing the geese overhead
>>> I looked up
> and saw what I thought was a flying saucer
>> above the town, bright white,   (5)
> with windows shimmering on the side.
>> Ah, it was gone
>>> before I could point out to my kind
>>> what flashed
> and stopped on a dime. How awful   (10)
>> to harbor a secret all your life,
>>> if only half believed,
>>> biting your lip
> to keep from screaming at everyone around,
>> "Do you know what I saw   (15)
> one night above the clouds?" A disc
>> of fire
>>> with the full moon lagging behind.

          Out there,
     where meteors collide and spaceships   (20)
          between one universe
 and the other abruptly pause, as if
     forbidden to satisfy
 a longing thought reserved for us,
     another God abides   (25)
     in love with silence. That night
          I saw
 His handiwork and was filled with awe
     that such a thing
     might be revealed to anyone like us,   (30)
     intent on seeking
 someone who'd look up before withdrawing
     into a darkness
 too vast to think about. I followed,
     coveting that dot   (35)
     that steered by starlight across the sky

     until it found at last
 a known ground, letting out souls
     that study each other
 with mercy that starts in the eyes.   (40)
     No doubt I should
 have shared this with someone wiser,
     but I was shy
     and too ashamed of whatever it was
 to confirm what I suddenly felt about human love.   (45)

EXPLORING VOCABULARY

List as many adjectives as possible to describe the speaker's feelings when he or she sees the flying saucer. Use a thesaurus if necessary.

PROFILING PHENOMENA

Using the profile sheet on page 156, write a profile of the phenomenon described in the poem. You may have to read between the lines—or

make inferences—to address some of the categories. When you are finished, discuss your answers with a small group of your peers or with the
entire class.

EXPLORING THE TEXT

1. How many sentences make up this poem?
2. What is the speaker's tone in this poem?
3. Why does Sampson break up the sentences the way he does?
4. Why is the left margin of the poem so irregular?

EXPLORING IDEAS

1. What does the speaker mean by "my kind" in line 8?
2. In the last stanza, the speaker tells the reader that he (or she) was "too ashamed of whatever it was/to confirm what I suddenly felt about human love." What do you think the speaker suddenly felt about human love?
3. What is the theme of the poem?
4. What does the reader know about the speaker?

Now Hear This: Shhhhhhhhh (Essay)

Jeanette Batz

PREREADING

Sit or stand in a public place—perhaps in front of your school—and record every sound that you hear for ten minutes. Next to each entry on your list, rate the sound in terms of loudness (1 = very low and 10 = very loud). Share your findings with the class.

ANNOTATING

While reading, underline any statistics offered by the author. In the margins, note your immediate reaction to reading the statistics.

When baby monkeys hear a clicking sound mimicking the beating of an owl's wings, they scamper instinctively to the ground. And when they hear a snakelike rustling, they climb into the trees. (1)

Like monkeys, humans are hardwired to react with alarm to loud, sudden, or shrill sounds, which start stress hormones pumping. Our ears, nerves, and internal organs take the hit. Nevertheless, we've got the microwave beeping, the smoke detector buzzing, fax-modems shrilling, and airplanes roaring. We shrug off the cacophony as modern life. (2)

Noise, one of our most pervasive and insidious pollutants, "is easy to ignore because it's invisible and transient. If your neighbor's playing his stereo at the threshold of pain, it may not happen again for a month, so you'll forget it. But your body remembers," remarks Ken Feith, U.S. Environmental Protection Agency (EPA) physicist. (3)

More than 20 million U.S. residents are exposed to enough environmental noise to damage their hearing, says the American

Speech-Language-Hearing Association (ASHA); 28 million have already suffered hearing loss. Studies have shown loss of libido due to intense noise, not to mention sleep deprivation; increases in blood pressure, pulse rate, and cholesterol and stress hormone levels; and deleterious effects on the respiratory, circulatory, digestive, and immune systems. In fact, drug companies use noise to test stress-reducing drugs.   (4)

The Reagan administration closed the EPA's Office of Noise Abatement and Control in 1982, calling noise a local problem. But rather than taking over noise-abatement activities, the states followed the fed's lead. About 1,100 local and state programs existed then; now there are fewer then 20. Community noise levels aren't regulated; most municipalities copy each other's inadequate ordinances. There are no federally funded educational programs or research, nor uniform product noise labeling.   (5)

The EPA must still enforce the 1972 Noise Control Act, a "shadow noise program," Feith laughingly calls it. "It's entirely unfunded, but I, for one, answer more than 1,000 calls a year." All Feith can do is offer unofficial suggestions. The stalled federal Quiet Communities Act of 1997 would reinstate the EPA's noise abatement office at about one-fourth its original budget, but activists want more.   (6)

Meanwhile, we let the military classify the results of their underwater sound experiments, and the Federal Aviation Administration (FAA) conduct their own noise studies, assuring us that "wildlife . . . rarely display any reactions to aviation noise"— completely ignoring all those squirrels with earplugs. ASHA claims that workplace noise regulation is lax; plant inspections are declining; and penalties for violating Occupational Safety and Health Administration (OSHA) noise standards are minimal. Even so, OSHA found 2,770 violations between 1995 and 1997, with $2 million in penalties.   (7)

How loud is too loud? Sound is measured in decibels, which increases logarithmically, so adding 10 decibels essentially doubles volume. A whisper is about 30; human voices 55 to 60. A jet takes off at 120 decibels. Feith cites a 20-year-old EPA study: "Above 55, the average person began to say, 'Gee, this is noisy'; at 65, most were prepared to . . . call the police. At 70, they were very upset. We now look at those three cutoffs as the maximum residential, commercial, and industrial levels, with a 10-decibel decrease in each at night."   (8)

Industry and transportation are the biggest noisemakers, generating more complaints than percussive neighbors. "We noise-pollute when we don't have direct contact with another human being," says Les Blomberg, director of the Noise Pollution Clearinghouse in Montpelier, Vermont. "In a car, someone may cut in front of you, but if you both walked up to a doorway at the same time, he would never hip-check you." And noise is spiraling: In 1995, auto traffic was up 262 percent from 1960, truck traffic 583 percent, passenger planes 538 percent, and air cargo (all those FedEx packages) 2,256 percent—at night.   (9)

According to ASHA, hearing loss can be caused by a single exposure to extremely loud noise, by repeated or long exposure to loud noise, or by extended exposure to moderate noise. Noise-induced hearing loss is gradual, painless, and permanent. First you have trouble understanding someone's remarks if there's background noise, then it's hard to distinguish words on the phone or at a meeting. Finally, it's tough to understand face-to-face conversations. You can still hear volume, but it's like listening to a blown speaker.   (10)

Hearing is a brain activity, linked to other systems. If you present a certain sound to a baby rat (apparently producing a short circuit during a critical brain-wiring period) then play it again 30 days later, the rat will have a seizure. Although our auditory wiring takes place in utero, the government got so excited by this phenomenon that during World War II they did research to see if they could make German troops drop their weapons.   (11)

A recent issue of *Journal of the American Medical Association* reported hearing loss—enough to affect speech perception, learning, self-image, and social skills—in almost 15 percent of children ages 6 to 19. New York psychologist Arlene Bronzaft found that kids in grades two to six whose classrooms were on the side of the school facing elevated train tracks were 11 months behind those on the quieter side in reading by their sixth year. After the New York City Transit Authority installed silencing equipment, a follow-up study showed no difference between the groups.   (12)

The Romans eventually banned chariots at night, but we'd rather die than ban our sport-utility vehicles. Rock 'n' roll takes the rap, but rock musicians—and listeners who enjoy their music—do not get as much hearing loss as industrial workers, says Dr. William Clark, who chairs Washington University's speech and hearing department. When his counterpart in Europe fed industrial noises through an amplifier in the same pattern and frequencies as rock music, the noise still caused more damage. (13)

Leaf blowers, especially commercial ones, which go above 115 decibels, are a different story. Even children's toys are problematic, given a toddler's tendency to hold the squeaker right next to her ear. And guns, with blasts that top 140 decibels, are the most important source of noise-induced hearing loss. (14)

Europeans are proof that we could create a quieter world. Their telephones and police alarms are gently singsong, not shrill; they research noise's physical and psychological effect (we focus only on hearing loss); and they refuse to buy our noisy products. Germany has planned new settlements with stringent noise protections; England spent more than 34 million pounds to insulate more than 50,000 dwellings from airport noise. The 1995 Environmental Report on China notes a $22.9 million investment in noise reduction (their noisiest city is Wenzhou, at 72.6 decibels). (15)

Then there's us. A former Toledo mayor's solution to airport noise was to move in people who were hard of hearing. Engineers can now make an acoustic mirror, creating peaks where there are valleys and valleys where there are peaks, so that mixing the two will silence the original noise. It's a start, along with handheld warning meters, baffles, barrier walls, and steel-mesh blankets hung over construction sites. (16)

We need narrower tires, and smaller, lighter cars. Roundabouts would avoid the shrieking of brakes and vroom of acceleration at intersections. Trucks could turn off their compression brakes and lower their backup-alarm volume. (17)

At home, sticking a mouse pad under the coffee grinder prevents turning the table into an amplifier. Keep the heirloom grandfather clock, but get rid of that cheap ticker in the corner. Control your environment—because industrial designers won't. Currently, the only mandatory noise labels are for hearing-protection devices. Fans and air conditioners have had noise labels for 25 years, but nobody knows what they mean. Finally, communities could make enforceable ordinances: "I tell them to bring a noise meter into the council hall," Blomberg says solemnly, "and bring in the Mothers of Invention, then

try to carry on their meeting at different decibel levels. They'll quickly
select 55 or lower, which is what the EPA found reasonable.   (18)

 Who knows, maybe they'd even be able to concentrate on public policy.   (19)

EXPLORING VOCABULARY

Look up the word *decibel* in a dictionary and an encyclopedia. Share the
information you discover with the class.

PROFILING PHENOMENA

Using the profile sheet on page 156, write a profile of the phenomenon
Batz describes. You may have to read between the lines—or make inferences—to address some of the categories. When you are finished, discuss
your answers with a small group of your peers or with the entire class.

EXPLORING THE TEXT

1. How do the statistics influence your reading of this essay? Do
   they make the author's points more believable? (Review your
   annotations.)
2. What is the author's main point? Is it explicit or implicit?
3. What is the author's purpose?
4. Is the author's introduction effective? Why or why not?

EXPLORING IDEAS

1. In paragraph eight, Batz asks the question: "How loud is too
   loud?" How does she answer that question? How would you answer that question?
2. In paragraph thirteen, Batz claims that "we'd rather die than ban
   our sport-utility vehicles." What does she mean? Do you agree or
   disagree? What other possessions or activities do we enjoy even
   though they may pose a threat to our hearing?
3. In paragraph eighteen, Batz tells us to control our environment.
   What can we do? Review her suggestions and then try to come
   up with a few of your own.
4. Why do many young people like loud music?

Hooked on Anger   (Essay)

RUSSELL BAKER

PREREADING

Make a list of things that make you angry. Then make a list of things that make you happy. Which list is longer? Why?

ANNOTATING

While reading, underline any points with which you strongly agree or strongly disagree. In the margins, explain why.

Anger has become the national habit. You see it on the sullen faces of the fashion models who have obviously been told that anger sells. It pours out of the radio all day. Washington journalism hams snarl and shout at each other on television. Generations exchange sneers on TV and printed page. Ordinary people abuse congressmen and president with shockingly personal insults. Rudeness is a justifiable way of showing you can no longer control the fury within. Vile speech, justified on the same ground, is inescapable.   (1)

America is angry at Washington, angry at the press, angry at immigrants, angry at television, angry at traffic, angry at people who are well off and angry at people who are poor, angry at blacks and angry at whites.   (2)

The old are angry at the young, the young angry at the old. Suburbs are angry at cities, cities are angry at suburbs, and rustic America is angry at both whenever urban and suburban intruders threaten the peaceful rustic sense of having escaped from God's Angry Land.   (3)

Enough: A complete catalog of the varieties of bile spoiling the American day would fill a library. The question is why. Why has anger become a reflexive response to the inevitable vagaries of national life?   (4)

Living perpetually at the boiling point seems to leave the country depressed and pessimistic. Study those scowling models wearing the latest clothes in the Sunday papers and magazines. Those are the faces that expect only the worst. What a pity to waste such lovely new clothes on people so incapable of happiness. (5)

The popularity of anger is doubly puzzling, not only because the American habit even in the worst of times has traditionally been mindless optimism, but also because there is relatively little nowadays for the nation to be angry about. (6)

The country re-elected President Eisenhower in 1956 because it believed his campaign boast about giving it peace and prosperity. The "peace," of course, was life under endless threat of nuclear devastation. (7)

By contrast the country now, at last, really does enjoy peace, and if the prosperity is not so solid as it was in the 1950s, American wealth is still the world's vastest. So, with real peace and prosperity, what's to be so furious about? (8)

The explanation, I suspect, is that the country got itself addicted to anger and can't shake the habit. It was hooked long ago when there was very good reason for anger. (9)

Massive, irritating and even scary expressions of anger—from Americans both black and white—were needed for the triumph of Martin Luther King and the civil rights movement. (10)

These were monumental victories. If the nation had been unwilling to get mad—to shout, "We're not going to take it anymore!"—they might not have been won. (11)

But what monumental struggle confronts us now? Giving young black people a stake in America is our most pressing problem, but nobody shouts much about that. Most other problems are so unmonumental that we might think the times ripe for greatness: an era of civility conducive to good feeling among neighbors of all races and persuasions, a golden age of progress in learning the arts and science. (12)

Is this making you angry? It's easy to imagine the cries of rage from people habituated to crying rage: Are women not still oppressed by glass ceilings? Do black Americans no longer have to suffer the disrespect of a racist world? Who dares talk of prosperity when the wealth is distributed so unfairly? (13)

True, all true. There is far too much poverty, racism remains an affliction, women still don't have economic equality with men. . . . (14)

Politically minded people concerned with these issues have always known that low-grade anger must be maintained, that political feet must be kept to the fire, that the squeaky wheel gets the grease, and so on. The high-intensity fury now seething through the land on these and a hundred other issues, however, doesn't seem focused on any social or economic goal. It's as though the nation got mad as hell a long time ago, got good results, and now can't shake the anger habit.   (15)

EXPLORING VOCABULARY

Find as many synonyms as possible for the words *anger* and *angry*. Which ones could be used in this essay without changing the meaning of the sentences?

PROFILING PHENOMENA

Using the profile sheet on page 156, write a profile of the phenomenon Baker describes. You may have to read between the lines—or make inferences—to address some of the categories. When you are finished, discuss your answers with a small group of your peers or with the entire class.

EXPLORING THE TEXT

1. What is the main idea? Is it implicit or explicit?
2. What techniques does Baker use to show transition between ideas?
3. What is Baker's tone?
4. Why does Baker ask us a question in paragraph four? Does he answer the question?

EXPLORING IDEAS

1. With which of Baker's ideas do you agree? With which do you disagree? Why? (Review your annotations.)
2. How much anger are you exposed to on a daily basis?
3. How much anger do you feel on a daily basis?
4. Can anger, as Baker suggests, be productive or constructive? Has anger ever been productive or constructive in your life? Explain.

The Tell-Tale Heart (Short Story)

Edgar Allan Poe

PREREADING

Do some research about Edgar Allan Poe's life and career. Share your findings with the class.

ANNOTATING

While reading, underline any words you do not understand. In the margins, try to define the words using context clues.

True!—nervous—very, very dreadfully nervous I had been and am; but why *will* you say that I am mad? The disease had sharpened my senses—not destroyed—not dulled them. Above all was the sense of hearing acute. I heard all things in the heaven and in the earth. I heard many things in hell. How, then, am I mad? Hearken! And observe how healthily—how calmly I can tell you the whole story.   (1)

It is impossible to say how the first idea entered my brain; but once conceived, it haunted me day and night. Object there was none. Passion there was none. I loved the old man. He had never wronged me. He had never given me insult. For his gold I had no desire. I think it was his eye! Yes, it was this! One of his eyes resembled that of a vulture—a pale blue eye, with a film over it. Whenever it fell upon me, my blood ran cold; and so by degrees—very gradually—I made up my mind to take the life of the old man, and thus rid myself of the eye forever.   (2)

Now this is the point. You fancy me mad. Madmen know nothing. But you should have seen *me*. You should have seen how wisely I proceeded—with what caution—with what foresight—with what dissimulation I went to work! I was never kinder to the old man than during the whole week before I killed him. And every night, about midnight, I turned the latch of his door and opened it—oh, so gently! And then, when I had made an opening sufficient for my head, I put in a dark lantern, all closed, closed, so that no light shone out, and then I thrust in my head. Oh, you would have laughed to see how cunningly I thrust it in! I moved it slowly—very, very slowly, so that I might not disturb the old man's sleep. It took me an hour to place my whole head within the opening so far that I could see him as he lay upon his bed. Ha—would a madman have been so wise as this? And then, when my head was well in the room, I undid the lantern cautiously—oh, so cautiously—cautiously (for the hinges creaked)—I undid it just so much that a single thin ray fell upon the vulture eye. And this I did for seven long nights—every night just after midnight— but I found the eye always closed; and so it was impossible to do the work; for it was not the old man who vexed me, but his Evil Eye. And every morning, when the day broke, I went boldly to the chamber, and spoke courageously to him, calling him by name in a hearty tone, and inquiring how he had passed the night. So you see he would have been a very profound old man, indeed, to suspect that every night, just at twelve, I looked in upon him while he slept. (3)

Upon the eighth night I was more than usually cautious in opening the door. A watch's minute hand moves more quickly than did mine. Never before that night had I *felt* the extent of my own powers—of my sagacity. I could scarcely contain my feelings of triumph. To think that there I was, opening the door, little by little, and he not even to dream of my secret deeds or thoughts. I fairly chuckled at the idea; and perhaps he heard me; for he moved on the bed suddenly, as if startled. Now you may think that I drew back—but no. His room was black as pitch with the thick darkness (for the shutters were close fastened, through fear of robbers), and so I knew that he could not see the opening of the door, and I kept pushing it on steadily, steadily. (4)

I had my head in, and was about to open the lantern, when my thumb slipped upon the tin fastening, and the old man sprang up in the bed, crying out—"Who's there?" I kept quite still and said nothing. For a whole hour I did not move a muscle, and in the meantime I did not hear him lie down. He was still sitting up in the bed listening;—just as I have done, night after night, hearkening to the death watches in the wall. (5)

Presently I heard a slight groan, and I knew it was the groan of mortal terror. It was not the groan of pain or of grief—oh, no!—it was the low stifled sound that arises from the bottom of the soul when overcharged with awe. I knew the sound well. Many a night, just at midnight, when all the world slept, it has welled up from my own bosom, deepening with its dreadful echo, the terrors that distracted me. I say I knew it well. I knew what the old man felt, and pitied him, although I chuckled at heart. I knew that he had been lying awake ever since the first slight noise, when he had turned in the bed. His fears had been ever since growing upon him. He had been trying to fancy them causeless, but could not. He had been saying to himself— "It is nothing but the wind in the chimney—it is only a mouse crossing the floor," or "it is merely a cricket which has made a single chirp." Yes, he had been trying to comfort himself with these suppositions; but he had found all in vain. *All in vain*; because Death, in approaching him, had stalked with his black shadow before him, and enveloped the victim. And it was the mournful influence of the unperceived shadow that caused him to feel—although he neither saw or heard—to *feel* the presence of my head in the room.   (6)

When I had waited a long time, very patiently, without hearing him lie down, I resolved to open a little—a very, very little crevice in the lantern. So I opened it—you cannot imagine how stealthily, stealthily—until, at length, a single dim ray, like the thread of a spider, shot from out the crevice and fell upon the vulture eye.   (7)

It was open—wide, wide open—and I grew furious as I gazed upon it. I saw it with perfect distinctness—all a dull blue, with a hideous veil over it that chilled the very marrow in my bones; but I could see nothing else of the old man's face or person: for I had directed the ray as if by instinct, precisely upon the damned spot.   (8)

And now have I not told you that what you mistake for madness is but over-acuteness of the senses?—now, I say, there came to my ears a low, dull, quick sound, such as a watch makes when enveloped in cotton. I knew *that* sound well too. It was the beating of the old man's heart. It increased my fury, as the beating of a drum stimulates the soldier into courage.   (9)

But even yet I refrained and kept still. I scarcely breathed. I held the lantern motionless. I tried how steadily I could maintain the ray upon the eye. Meantime the hellish tattoo of the heart increased. It grew quicker and quicker, and louder and louder every instant. The old man's terror *must* have been extreme! It grew louder, I say, louder every moment!—do you mark me well? I have told you that I am nervous: so I am. And now at the dead hour of the night, amid the dreadful silence of that old house, so strange a noise as this excited me to uncontrollable terror. Yet, for some minutes longer I refrained and stood still. But the beating grew louder, louder! I thought the heart must burst. And now a new anxiety seized me—the sound would be heard by a neighbor! The old man's hour had come! With a loud yell, I threw open the lantern and leaped into the room. He shrieked once—once only. In an instant, I dragged him to the floor, and pulled the heavy bed over him. I then smiled gaily, to find the deed so far done. But, for many minutes, the heart beat on with a muffled sound. This, however, did not vex me; it would not be heard through the wall. At length it ceased. The old man was dead. I removed the bed and examined the corpse. Yes, he was stone, stone dead. I placed my hand upon the heart and held it there many minutes. There was no pulsation. He was stone dead. His eye would trouble me no more.   (10)

If still you think me mad, you will think so no longer when I describe the wise precautions I took for the concealment of the body. The night waned, and I worked hastily, but in silence. First of all I dismembered the corpse. I cut off the head and the arms and the legs.   (11)

I then took up three planks from the flooring of the chamber, and deposited all between the scantlings. I then replaced the boards so cleverly, so cunningly, that no human eye—not even *his*—could have detected anything wrong. There was nothing to wash out—no stain of any kind—no blood spot whatever. I had been too wary for that. A tub had caught all—ha! ha!   (12)

When I had made an end of these labors, it was four o'clock—still dark as midnight. As the bell sounded the hour, there came a knocking at the street door. I went down to open it with a light heart—for what had I *now* to fear? There entered three men, who introduced themselves, with perfect suavity, as officers of the police. A shriek had been heard by a neighbor during the night; suspicion of foul play had been aroused; information had been lodged at the police office, and they (the officers) had been deputed to search the premises.   (13)

I smiled—for *what* had I to fear? I bade the gentlemen welcome. The shriek, I said, was my own in a dream. The old man, I mentioned was absent in the country. I took my visitors all over the house. I bade them search—search *well*. I led them, at length, to *his* chamber. I showed them his treasures, secure, undisturbed. In the enthusiasm of my confidence, I brought chairs into the room, and desired them here to rest from their fatigues, while I myself, in the wild audacity of perfect triumph, placed my own seat upon the very spot beneath which reposed the corpse of the victim. (14)

The officers were satisfied. My *manner* had convinced them. I was singularly at ease. They sat, and while I answered cheerily, they chatted familiar things. But, ere long, I felt myself getting pale and wished them gone. My head ached, and I fancied a ringing in my ears: but still they sat and still chatted. The ringing became more distinct:—it continued and became more distinct: I talked more freely to get rid of the feeling: but it continued and gained definiteness—until, at length, I found that the noise was not within my ears. (15)

No doubt I now grew *very* pale;—but I talked more fluently, and with a heightened voice. Yet the sound increased—and what could I do? It was a *low, dull, quick sound—much such a sound as a watch makes when enveloped in cotton.* I gasped for breath—and yet the officers heard it not. I talked more quickly—more vehemently; but the noise steadily increased. I arose and argued about trifles, in a high key and with violent gesticulations, but the noise steadily increased. Why *would* they not be gone? I paced the floor to and fro with heavy strides, as if excited to fury by the observation of the men—but the noise steadily increased. Oh God! what *could* I do? I foamed—I raved—I swore! I swung the chair upon which I had been sitting, and grated it upon the boards, but the noise arose over all and continually increased. It grew louder—louder—*louder!* And still the men chatted pleasantly, and smiled. Was it possible they heard it not? Almighty God!—no, no! They heard!—they suspected!—they knew!—they were making a mockery of my horror!—this I thought, and this I think, But anything was better than this agony! Any thing was more tolerable than this derision! I could bear the hypocritical smiles no longer! I felt that I must scream or die!—and now—again!—hark! louder! louder! louder! *louder!*— (16)

"Villains!" I shrieked, "dissemble no more! I admit the deed!—tear up the planks!—here, here!—it is the beating of his hideous heart!" (17)

EXPLORING VOCABULARY

Make a list of the words you underlined and tried to define using context clues. (Review your annotations.) Check your definitions with dictionary definitions. Share your findings with the class.

PROFILING PHENOMENA

Using the profile sheet on page 156, write a profile of the phenomenon the narrator describes. You may have to read between the lines—or make inferences—to address some of the categories. When you are finished, discuss your answers in small groups or with the entire class.

EXPLORING THE TEXT

1. From whose point of view is this story told?
2. What is the narrator's tone? Do you find the tone appealing?
3. Why does Poe use so many dashes in this story?
4. Why are certain words in the story italicized?

EXPLORING IDEAS

1. What was your immediate reaction to Poe's story?
2. What is the significance of the title?
3. How would you describe the narrator? Why?
4. Reread paragraph five. What does the narrator mean by "death watches in the wall"?
5. Does this story have a theme?

The Right Chemistry (ESSAY)

ANASTASIA TOUFEXIS

PREREADING

The following essay begins with an epigraph (a quotation at the beginning of a work that is meant to shed some insight on the work). Read the epigraph at the beginning of this work and then free write about what it means and what it tells you about the essay.

ANNOTATING

While reading, underline any idea that seems to contradict what you believe about love. In the margins, make a brief note of your beliefs.

Love is a romantic designation for a most ordinary biological—or, shall we say, chemical?—process. A lot of nonsense is talked and written about it.

> -*Greta Garbo to Melvyn Douglas in* Ninotchka

O.K., let's cut out all this nonsense about romantic love. Let's bring some scientific precision to the party. Let's put love under a microscope. (1)

When rigorous people with Ph.D.s after their names do that, what they see is not some silly, senseless thing. No, their probe reveals that love rests firmly on the foundations of evolution, biology, and chemistry. What seems on the surface to be irrational, intoxicated behavior is in fact part of nature's master strategy—a vital force that has helped humans survive, thrive, and multiply through thousands of years. Says Michael Mille, a psychology professor at Loyola Marymount University in Los Angeles: "Love is our ancestors whispering in our ears." (2)

It was on the plains of Africa about 4 million years ago, in the early days of the human species, that the notion of romantic love probably first began to blossom—or at least that the first cascades of neurochemicals began flowing from the brain to the bloodstream to produce goofy grins and sweaty palms as men and women gazed deeply into each other's eyes. When mankind graduated from scuttling around on all fours to walking on two legs, this change made the whole person visible to fellow human beings for the first time. Sexual organs were in full display, as were other characteristics, from the color of eyes to the span of shoulders. As never before, each individual had a unique allure. (3)

When the sparks flew, new ways of making love enabled sex to become a romantic encounter, not just a reproductive act. Although mounting mates from the rear was, and still is, the method favored among most animals, humans began to enjoy face-to-face couplings; both looks and personal attraction became a much greater part of the equation. (4)

Romance served the evolutionary purpose of pulling males and females into long-term partnership, which was essential to child rearing. On open grasslands, one parent would have a hard—and dangerous—time handling a child while foraging for food. "If a woman was carrying the equivalent of a 20 lb. bowling ball in one arm and a pile of sticks in the other, it was ecologically critical to pair up with a mate to rear the young," explains anthropologist Helen Fisher, author of *Anatomy of Love*. (5)

While Western culture holds fast to the idea that true love flames forever (the movie *Bram Stoker's Dracula* has the Count carrying the torch beyond the grave), nature apparently meant passions to sputter out in something like four years. Primitive pairs stayed together just "long enough to rear one child through infancy," says Fisher. Then each would find a new partner and start all over again. (6)

What Fisher calls the "four-year itch" shows up unmistakably in today's divorce statistics. In most of the 62 cultures she has studied, divorce rates peak around the fourth year of marriage. Additional youngsters help keep pairs together longer. If, say, a couple have another child three years after the first, as often occurs, then their union can be expected to last about four more years. That makes them ripe for the more familiar phenomenon in the Marilyn Monroe classic *The Seven-Year Itch*. (7)

If, in nature's design, romantic love is not eternal, neither is it exclusive. Less than 5% of mammals form rigorously faithful pairs. From the earliest days, contends Fisher, the human pattern has been "monogamy with clandestine adultery." Occasional flings upped the chances that new combinations of genes would be passed on to the next generation. Men who sought new partners had more children. Contrary to common assumptions, women were just as likely to stray. "As long as prehistoric females were secretive about their extramarital affairs," argues Fisher, "they could garner extra resources, life insurance, better genes and more varied DNA for their biological futures. . . ."   (8)

Lovers often claim that they feel as if they are being swept away. They're not mistaken; they are literally flooded by chemicals, research suggests. A meeting of eyes, a touch of hands or a whiff of scent sets off a flood that starts in the brain and races along the nerves through the blood. The results are familiar: flushed skin, sweaty palms, heavy breathing. If love looks suspiciously like stress, the reason is simple: the chemical pathways are identical.   (9)

Above all, there is the sheer euphoria of falling in love—a not-so-surprising reaction, considering many of the substances swamping the newly smitten are chemical cousins of amphetamines. They include dopamine, norepinephrine, and especially phenylethylamine (PEA). Cole Porter knew what he was talking about when he wrote "I get a kick out of you." "Love is a natural high," observes Anthony Walsh, author of *The Science of Love: Understanding Love and Its Effects on Mind and Body*. "PEA gives you that silly smile that you flash at strangers. When we meet someone who is attractive to us, the whistle blows at the PEA factory."   (10)

But phenylethylamine highs don't last forever, a fact that lends support to arguments that passionate romantic love is short-lived. As with any amphetamine, the body builds up a tolerance to PEA; thus it takes more and more of the substance to produce love's special kick. After two to three years, the body simply can't crank up the needed amount of PEA. And chewing on chocolate doesn't help, despite popular belief. The candy is high in PEA, but it fails to boost the body's supply.   (11)

Fizzling chemicals spell the end of delirious passion; for many people that marks the end of the liaison as well. It is particularly true for those whom Dr. Michael Liebowitz of the New York State

Psychiatric Institute terms "attraction junkies." They crave the intoxication of falling in love so much that they move frantically from affair to affair just as soon as the first rush of infatuation fades.   (12)

Still, many romances clearly endure beyond the first years. What accounts for that? Another set of chemicals, of course. The continued presence of partner gradually steps up production in the brain of endorphins. Unlike the fizzy amphetamines, these are soothing substances. Natural pain-killers, they give lovers a sense of security, peace, and calm. "That is one reason why it feels so horrible when we're abandoned or a lover dies," notes Fisher. "We don't have our daily hit of narcotics."   (13)

Researchers see a contrast between the heated infatuation induced by PEA, along with other amphetamine-like chemicals, and the more intimate attachment fostered and prolonged by endorphins. "Early love is when you love the way the other person makes you feel," explains psychiatrist Mark Goulston of the University of California, Los Angeles. "Mature love is when you love the person as he or she is." It is the difference between passionate and compassionate love, observes Walsh, a psychobiologist at Boise State University in Idaho. "It's Bon Jovi vs. Beethoven."   (14)

Oxytocin is another chemical that has recently been implicated in love. Produced by the brain, it sensitizes nerves and stimulates muscle contraction during childbirth as well as the production of breast milk, and seems to inspire mothers to nuzzle their infants. Scientists speculate that oxytocin might encourage similar cuddling between adult women and men. The versatile chemical may also enhance orgasms. In one study of men, oxytocin increased three to five times its normal level during climax, and it may soar even higher in women.   (15)

Chemicals may help explain (at least to scientists) the feelings of passion and compassion, but why do people tend to fall in love with one partner rather than a myriad of others? Once again, it's partly a function of evolution and biology. "Men are looking for maximal fertility in a mate," says Loyola Marymount's Mills. "That is in large part why females in the prime childbearing ages of 17–28 are so desirable." Men can size up youth and vitality in a glance, and studies indeed show that men fall in love quite rapidly. Women tumble more slowly, to a large degree because their requirements are more complex; they need more time to check the guy out. "Age is not vital," notes

Mills, "but the ability to provide security, father children, share resources and hold a high status in society are all key factors." (16)

Still, that does not explain why the way Mary walks and laughs makes Bill dizzy with desire while Marcia's gait and giggle leave him cold. "Nature has wired us for one special person," suggests Walsh romantically. He rejects the idea that a woman or a man can be in love with two people at the same time. Each person carries in his or her mind a unique subliminal guide to the ideal partner, a "love map," to borrow a term coined by sexologist John Money of Johns Hopkins University. (17)

Drawn from the people and experiences of childhood, the map is a record of whatever we found enticing and exciting—or disturbing and disgusting. Small feet, curly hair. The way our mothers patted our head or how our fathers told a joke. A fireman's uniform, a doctor's stethoscope. All the information gathered while growing up is imprinted in the brain's circuitry by adolescence. Partners never meet each and every requirement, but a sufficient number of matches can light up the wires and signal, "It's love." Not every partner will be like the last one, since lovers may have different combinations of characteristics favored by the map. (18)

O.K., that's the scientific point of view. Satisfied? Probably not. To most people—with or without Ph.D.s—love will always be more than the sum of its natural parts. It's a commingling of body and soul, reality and imagination, poetry and phenylethylamine. In our deepest hearts, most of us harbor the hope that love will never fully yield up its secrets, that it will always elude our grasp. (19)

EXPLORING VOCABULARY

Toufexis uses a great deal of scientific terminology in this essay. Make a list of all the scientific words she uses and see if you can identify any of the word parts listed on page 203.

PROFILING PHENOMENA

Using the profile sheet on page 156, write a profile of the phenomenon Toufexis describes. You may have to read between the lines—or make inferences—to address some of the categories. When you are finished, discuss your answers with a small group of your peers or with the entire class.

EXPLORING THE TEXT

1. What is Toufexis's tone in this article? Does she have more than one tone? Which tone is predominant?
2. Who is the intended audience for this piece? How do you know?
3. Reread Toufexis's introduction and conclusion. How are they similar? Do their similarities make this essay more engaging or effective?
4. Do you think the information in the article is reliable? Why or why not?

EXPLORING IDEAS

1. What is Toufexis's main point? Do you agree or disagree with her main point? Why?
2. How do you view love? How do you think love originated?
3. What kinds of love—other than romantic love—exist? Of those, which can be understood through body chemistry?
4. Do you look to science for the answers to your questions about life, love, and relationships? If not, where do you look?
5. How does your idea of love compare or contrast with the author's? (Review your annotations.)

Health Watch: Eating Disorders— Betrayal of the Body (TEXTBOOK EXCERPT)

TERESA AUDESIRK AND GERALD AUDESIRK

PREREADING

Go to the library with a group of your classmates and look through several popular women's magazines and men's magazines. Count the number of articles and advertisements you find pertaining to weight loss. Do the magazines geared toward men or those geared toward women contain more ads or articles about dieting? If there are differences, what is the significance of those differences? Share your findings with the rest of the class.

ANNOTATING

While reading, underline any information that you think might appear on a test if you were reading this for a biology class. In the margins, note why you think so.

Food is a fundamental requirement of all animals; no animal can survive without eating. Natural selection has therefore provided animals with mechanisms to ensure that the impulse to eat arises when nutrients are needed. In humans, however, these natural impulses, so crucial to our health and well-being, can go terribly awry. In recent decades we have seen an increase in the occurrence of *eating disorders*, ailments characterized by the disruption of normal eating behavior.   (1)

Eating disorders include two particularly debilitating illnesses, *anorexia nervosa* and *bulimia nervosa*. People with anorexia nervosa experience an intense fear of gaining weight, and they achieve extreme weight loss by eating very little food. This drastically reduced eating is commonly accompanied by other measures, including self-induced vomiting, laxative intake, and excessive exercise. The consequences of the behaviors associated with anorexia nervosa are disastrous. Anorexics become emaciated, losing both fat and muscle mass. This emaciation can in turn disrupt cardiac, digestive, endocrine, and reproductive functions. Up to 18% of anorexics die as a result of their disorder.   (2)

The main symptom of bulimia nervosa is recurrent bouts of binge eating, in which extraordinarily large amounts of food are consumed in a short period. The binge eating of bulimics is typically followed by the same kinds of purging behaviors common in anorexics, such as vomiting and laxative consumption. In most cases the health consequences of bulimia nervosa are not as dire as those of anorexia nervosa, because there is no drastic weight loss.   (3)

Girls and young women are most at risk for eating disorders. More than 90% of diagnosed eating disorders occur in females; in the large majority of these cases, onset of the illness takes place between 13 and 20 years of age. The causes of eating disorders are not well understood. In a body wracked by the near-starvation of anorexia nervosa, the effects of the illness are hard to distinguish from a defect that might be a cause. No clear genetic link to the disorders has been found thus far, so suspicion has fallen on environmental factors, especially on societal pressures to be thin.   (4)

Unfortunately, existing treatments for eating disorders are not terribly effective. The most common treatment, hospitalization (to restore nutritional health) and counseling, does not typically lead to full recovery. Antidepressant drugs are helpful in some cases but are more likely to be effective for bulimia nervosa than for the more dire anorexia nervosa. Hope may be on the horizon, however, owing to a recent explosion of research findings about the hormones that control appetite. For example, researchers have discovered a class of hormones known as orexins (from the Greek word *orexis*, meaning "appetite"), which, when injected into mice, bind receptors in the brain and cause food consumption to increase dramatically. Such new discoveries raise hope that as our understanding of the physiological control of appetite grows, we may yet be able to devise chemical treatments for eating disorders.   (5)

EXPLORING VOCABULARY

Look up the terms *anorexia nervosa* and *bulimia nervosa* and find the origins of the words. How are the original meanings similar or different from the modern meanings?

PROFILING PHENOMENA

Using the profile sheet on page 156, write a profile of the phenomenon the Audesirks describe. You may have to read between the lines—or make inferences—to address some of the categories. When you are finished, discuss your answers with a small group of your peers or with the entire class.

EXPLORING THE TEXT

1. What is the main idea?
2. What is the purpose?
3. Does the information in the excerpt seem reliable? Why or why not?
4. What conclusions, if any, do the authors draw about eating disorders?

EXPLORING IDEAS

1. Why do you think that anorexia and bulimia primarily affect young women?
2. Do you know anyone with an eating disorder? If so, how does the disorder affect your relationship with that person?
3. After reading the excerpt, do you think eating disorders are psychological or physiological? Why?
4. Does the media contribute to eating disorders? (Refer to your research.)
5. What information from the excerpt might appear on a test in a biology class? (Review your annotations.)

Fear Not! (ESSAY)

JEFFREY KLUGER

PREREADING

Free write about something that causes you to feel fear. It could be a certain natural phenomenon, a type of animal, or a particular social situation. Consider why you feel the fear.

ANNOTATING

While reading, underline any ideas or information that seem to explain the fear about which you wrote.

It's not easy moving through the world when you're terrified of electricity. "Donna," 45, a writer, knows that better than most. Get her in the vicinity of an appliance or a light switch or—all but unthinkable—a thunderstorm, and she is overcome by a terror so blinding she can think of nothing but fleeing. That, of course, is not always possible, so over time, Donna has come up with other answers. When she opens the refrigerator door, rubber-soled shoes are a must. If a light bulb blows, she will tolerate the dark until someone else changes it for her. Clothes shopping is done only when necessary, lest static on garments send her running from the store. And swimming at night is absolutely out of the question, lest underwater lights electrocute her. When there's a possibility that lightning may strike, she simply shuts everything off in her house and sits alone in a darkened room until the danger passes. (1)

There is a word—a decidedly straightforward one—for Donna's condition: *electrophobia*, or a morbid fear of electricity. . . . (2)

For every phobia the infinitely inventive—and infinitely fearful—human mind can create, there is a word that has been coined to describe it. There's *nephophobia*, or fear of clouds, and *coulrophobia*, the fear of clowns. There's *kathisophobia*, fear of sitting, and *kyphophobia*, fear of stooping. There are *xanthophobia, leukophobia,* and *chromophobia*, fear of yellow, white and colors in general. There are *alektorophobia* and *apiphobia*, fear of chickens and bees. And deep in the list, lost in the *L*s, there's *lutraphobia*, or fear of otters—a fear that's useful, it would seem, only if you happen to be a mollusk.

(3)

The list of identified phobias is expanding every day and is now, of course, collected online (www.phobialist.com), where more than 500 increasingly quirky human fears are labeled, sometimes tongue-in-cheek, and catalogued alphabetically. Some have more to do with neology than psychology. (It's one thing to invent a word like *arachibutyrophobia*, another thing to find someone who's really afraid of peanut butter sticking to the roof of the mouth.) Other phobias, however—like *acrophobia* (fear of heights), *claustrophobia* (fear of enclosed spaces) and *agoraphobia* (a crushing, paralyzing terror of anything outside the safety of home)—can be deadly serious business.

(4)

If the names of phobias can be found online, the people who actually suffer from at least one of them at some point in their life—about 50 million in the U.S. by some estimates—are everywhere. They may be like "Beth," a pseudonym, a middle school student in Boston whose hemophobia, or fear of blood, was so severe that even a figure of speech like "cut it out" could make her faint. Or they may be like "Jean," 38, an executive assistant in New Jersey who is so terrified of balloons that just walking into a birthday party can make her break out in a sweat. . . .

(5)

For something that can cause as much suffering as a phobia, it's remarkable how many people lay claim to having one—and how many of them are wrong. Self-described computer phobics are probably nothing of the kind. They may not care for the infernal machines and may occasionally want to throw one out the window, but that's not the same as a full-fledged phobia. Self-described claustrophobics often misdiagnose as well. The middle seat on a transatlantic flight may be something you approach with dismay, but unless you also experience a racing heart and ragged breath, you are probably not phobic. Drawing the distinction between distaste and the singular terror of a phobia is not always easy—and it's made all the harder by the fact that fear in some circumstances is perfectly appropriate. If flying into a storm or

easing into weaving traffic isn't the right time to go a little white
knuckled, what is? (6)

Experts, however, say a true phobic reaction is a whole different
category of terror, a central nervous system wildfire that's impossible to
mistake. In the face of the thing that triggers fear, phobics experience
sweating, racing heart, difficulty breathing and even a fear of imminent
death—all accompanied by an overwhelming need to flee. In addition,
much of the time that they are away from the feared object or
situation is spent dreading the next encounter and developing
elaborate strategies intended to avoid it. "Jeanette," 44, a teacher's
assistant, is so terrified of cats that she sends her daughter, 21, into an
unfamiliar store to scout around and sound a feline all clear before she
enters. The daughter has been walking point this way since age five.
"Nora," 50, a social worker, will circumnavigate a block with a series
of right turns rather than making a single left, so afraid is she of facing
the stream of traffic that a left turn requires. (7)

Most psychologists now assign phobias to one of three broad
categories: social phobias, in which the sufferer feels paralyzing fear at
the prospect of social or professional encounters; panic disorders, in
which a person is periodically blindsided by overwhelming fear for no
apparent reason; and specific phobias—fear of snakes and enclosed
spaces and the like. Of the three, the specific phobias are the easiest to
treat, partly because they are the easiest to understand. . . . (8)

Contemporary researchers believe it's no coincidence that specific
phobias usually fall into one of the four subcategories, all of which
would have had meaning to our ancient ancestors: fear of insects or
animals; fear of natural environments, like heights and the dark; fear of
blood or injury; and fear of dangerous situations, like being trapped in
a tight space. "Phobias are not random," says Michelle Craske,
psychologist at UCLA's Anxiety and Behavioral Disorders Program.
"We tend to fear anything that threatens our survival as a species."
When times change, new fears develop, but the vast majority still fit
into one of the four groups. (9)

It turns out that we process the fear of these modern menaces in
the same area of the brain our ancient ancestors did—the paralimbic
region, which mediates a whole range of primal responses, including
anger and sexual arousal. "It seems that contemporary people learned
from their ancient ancestors what to be afraid of and how to handle
it," Barlow says. (10)

Not all of us, however, parlay that ancient history into a modern-day phobia. It may be our distant ancestors who predispose us to phobias, but its our immediate ancestors—specifically our parents—who seal the deal. As many as 40% of all people suffering from a specific phobia have at least one phobic parent, seemingly a clue that phobias could be genetically influenced. In recent years, a number of scientists have claimed to have found the phobia gene, but none of those claims have held up to scrutiny. If phobias are genetically based at all, they almost certainly require a whole tangle of genes to get the process going.   (11)

But genetics doesn't even have to be involved as long as learning is. A childhood trauma—a house fire, say, or a dog bite—may be more than enough to seize the brain's attention and serve as a repository for incipient fears. "Temperament also seems to be critical," says Craske. "Two people can go through the exact same traumatic event, but the high-strung, emotionally sensitive person is more vulnerable to the fear." Even secondhand fears—watching Mom or Dad react with exaggerated terror to a cockroach or a drop of blood, for example, may play a role. The journal *Nature* last week reported a study in which researchers performed scans on the fear centers of volunteer's brains and found that when the subjects were merely told to expect an electric shock, the neurological reaction to the anticipated jolt was as powerful as fears based on actual experience. "There is a lot of legitimacy to the idea that phobias can be learned," says Edna B. Foa, professor of psychology and psychiatry at the University of Pennsylvania. "We respond to what we see or experience."   (12)

In many cases, the brain may think it's doing the child a favor by developing a phobia. The world is a scary place, and young kids are inherently fearful until they start to figure it out. If you are living with a generalized sense of danger, it can be profoundly therapeutic to find a single object on which to deposit all that unformed fear—a snake, a spider, a rat. A specific phobia becomes a sort of backfire for fear, a controlled blaze that prevents other blazes from catching. "The thinking mind seeks out a rationale for the primitive mind's unexplained experiences," says psychologist Steven Phillipson, clinical director of the Center for Cognitive-Behavioral Psychotherapy in New York City.   (13)

But a condition that is so easy to pick up is becoming almost as easy to shake, usually without resort to drugs. What turns up the wattage of a phobia the most is the strategy that phobics rely on to ease their discomfort: avoidance. The harder phobics work to avoid the things they fear, the more the brain grows convinced that the threat is real. "The things you do to reduce anxiety just make it worse," says Barlow. "We have to strip those things away." (14)

And that's what doctors do. A patient visiting Barlow's Boston clinic is first assessed for the presence of a specific phobia and then guided through an intensive day or two of graduated exposure. People who are afraid of syringes and blood, for example, may first be shown a magazine photo with a trace of blood depicted in it. Innocuous photos give way to graphic photos, and graphic ones to a display of a real, empty syringe. Over time, the syringe is brought closer, and the patient learns to hold it and even tolerate having blood drawn. (15)

None of this is remotely easy for the phobic person, and the body's anxiety Klaxons may go off the instant the therapy begins. Gradually, however, as each exposure level is reached, the alarms start to quiet; they sound again only when the intensity of the exposure is turned up. "Just as people become habituated to the noise of traffic or background chatter, so too can phobics become nonresponsive to the things that once frightened them," says Phillipson. (16)

With that habituation comes profound recovery. In studies recently conducted by Lars Goran Ost, a psychology professor at Stockholm University and one of the pioneers of one-day phobia treatments, a staggering 80% to 95% of patients get their phobias under control after just one session. And when symptoms disappear, they usually stay gone. Patients, he says, rarely experience a significant phobic relapse, and almost never replace the thing they no longer fear with a fresher phobia object. . . . (17)

If specific phobias were the only type of phobias around, things would be decidedly easier for doctors and patients. But the two other members of the phobia troika—social phobias and panic disorders—can be a little bit trickier. (18)

Of the 50 million Americans who have experienced or will someday suffer from a phobia (and many will have more than one), 35 million will suffer from social phobia, and the battle they fight is a harrowing one. Richard Heimberg at Temple University's Adult Anxiety Clinic often thinks of the 50-year-old patient who talked frequently about getting married and having a family—a reasonable dream, except his terror of rejection had kept him from ever going out

on a date. After much encouragement and counseling, he finally
screwed up his courage enough to ask a woman out. The next day,
when Heimberg asked him if he'd had a good time, he said yes. But
when he asked if he were going to invite her out again, the patient
slumped and said no. "She's only going to give to charity once," he
explained.   (19)

For this patient, the problem wasn't mere low self-esteem but
outright terror. To a social phobic, the mere prospect of a social
encounter is frightening enough to cause sweating, trembling, light-
headedness and nausea, accompanied by an overwhelming feeling of
inadequacy. For some sufferers, the disorder is comparatively
circumscribed—occurring only at large parties, say—making avoidance
strategies seem easy. But social phobias can encroach into more and
more areas of life, closing more and more doors. As sufferers grow
increasingly isolated, they grow increasingly hopeless and risk
developing such conditions as depression and alcoholism.   (20)

But things don't have to be so bleak. While social phobias do not
respond to a single intensive exposure session as specific phobias do,
therapy can still be relatively straightforward. A successful treatment
regimen may involve no more than a dozen sessions of cognitive-
behavioral therapy, in which patients slowly expose themselves to the
places and circumstances that frighten them and reframe the
catastrophic thinking that torments them. They are taught to tone
down their "attentional bias," a tendency to stress their supposed social
stumbles, and their "interpretation bias," a habit of picking up neutral
cues from other people and interpreting them as evidence of failing
socially. Often group therapy works better than one-on-one therapy. It
provides more than a supportive circle of fellow sufferers; the very act
of gathering with other people can serve as a first, critical rebellion
against the disorder.   (21)

If such therapy doesn't help social phobics, drugs can. Ever since the
popularization of Prozac in the early 1990s, the family of modern
psychopharmacological drugs has grown steadily. Most of these
medications are selective serotonin reuptake inhibitors—or SSRIS—
which, as the name implies, selectively block the brain's reabsorption of
the neurotransmitter serotonin, helping produce feelings of satisfaction
and kick-start recovery. Last year the drug manufacturer Smith Kline
Beecham asked the Food and Drug Administration to take a second

look at the popular SSRI Paxil and consider approving it specifically for the treatment of social-anxiety disorder. The FDA agreed, making Paxil the first drug ever to be formally endorsed for such use.   (22)

While the flood of marketing tends to overstate the case, the fact is, Paxil works—not by eliminating anxiety entirely but by controlling it enough for traditional therapy to take hold. And with the pharmacological door now open, makers of similar drugs like Luvox, Prozac and Celexa will probably seek the same certification. "Paxil is not unique among these drugs," says Barlow. "It was just first in line."   (23)

Progress in treating social-anxiety disorder is also providing hope for the last—and most disabling—of the family of phobias: panic disorder. Panic disorder is to anxiety conditions what a tornado is to weather conditions: a devastating sneak attack that appears from nowhere, wreaks havoc and then simply vanishes. Unlike the specific phobic and the social phobic who know what will trigger their fear, the victim of panic attacks never knows where or when one will hit. Someone who experiences an attack in, say, a supermarket will often not return there, associating the once neutral place with the traumatic event. But the perceived circle of safety can quickly shrink, until sufferers may be confined entirely to their homes. When this begins to happen panic disorder mutates into full-blown agoraphobia. "For some people, even the house becomes too big," says Fordham University psychology professor Dean McKay. "They may limit their world to just a few rooms."   (24)

The treatment for agoraphobia is much the same as it is for social phobia: cognitive-behavioral therapy and drugs. In many cases, recovery takes longer than it does for social phobias because agoraphobic behavior can become so entrenched. Nonetheless, once therapy and drug treatment get under way, they sometimes move surprisingly quickly. "The best way to treat agoraphobia," says Ost, "is by individual therapy, once a week for 10 or 12 weeks."   (25)

If science has so many phobias on the run, does that mean that the problem as a whole can soon be considered solved? Hardly. Like all other emotional disorders, phobias cause a double dip of psychic pain: from the condition and from the shame of having the problem in the first place. Over the years, researchers have made much of the fact that the large majority of phobia sufferers are women—from 55% for social phobias and up to 90% for specific phobias and extreme cases of agoraphobia. Hormones, genes, and culture have all been explored as explanations. But the simplest answer may be that women own up to the condition more readily than men do. If you don't come forward with your problem, you can't be included in the epidemiologists' count. Worse, you can never avail yourself to the therapists' cure. . . .   (26)

The fact that phobias, of all the anxiety disorders, can be overcome so readily is one of psychology's brightest bits of clinical news in a long time. Phobias can beat the stuffing out of sufferers because the feelings they generate seem so real and the dangers they warn of so great. Most of the time, however, the dangers are mere neurochemical lies—and the lies have to be exposed. "Your instincts tell you to escape or avoid," says Phillipson. "But what you really need to do is face down the fear." When you spend your life in a cautionary crouch, the greatest relief of all may come from simply standing up.   (27)

EXPLORING VOCABULARY

Look up the words *phobia* and *fear*. What distinctions can be made between these two words?

PROFILING PHENOMENA

Using the profile sheet on page 156, write a profile of the phenomenon described by Kluger. You may have to read between the lines—or make inferences—to address some of the categories. When you are finished, discuss your answers with a small group of your peers or with the entire class.

EXPLORING THE TEXT

1. What is the purpose of this piece?
2. Why does Kluger include specific cases of people with phobias?
3. Why does the author put the names of people with particular phobias in quotation marks?

EXPLORING IDEAS

1. What are the three types of phobias discussed in the essay? How are they similar, and how are they different?
2. According to the author, what are the causes of phobias?

3. Do any of the causes of phobias set forth by Kluger explain the fear about which you wrote before reading this work? (Review your annotations.)

4. Do you know anyone who lives with a true phobia? How does this phobia affect his or her life?

Childless . . . with Children (ESSAY)

ANDY STEINER

PREREADING

With a group of your classmates, consider the following question: Why do people have children? Share your findings with the class.

ANNOTATING

While reading, underline information that the author based upon research. In the margins, note the type of research he did (interviews, reading, etc.).

Cynthia Scott and her partner, Cathy Hoffman, have attended two births. They're not midwives, or mothers, or even doting aunts. They're godmothers, but not in the traditional sense of the word. (1)

"I met Suzanne and Doug in 1985," recalls Scott, who lives in Minneapolis. "They had their first daughter, Hannah, in 1987. They asked Cathy and me to be godmothers before Hannah was even born. They also asked us to be present at her birth. At the time, they didn't know exactly what the term *godmother* meant to them, except that they wanted us to be part of their future children's lives. It wasn't about teaching the rosary or taking them to Sunday school or anything like that. It was more like being a second set of parents. (2)

Hannah's birth was followed three years later by the birth of her sister, Natalie, which Hoffman and Scott also attended. In the years since, they've become a presence in both girls' lives, providing extra help for their exhausted parents when the girls were babies, hosting them for weekend overnights as they got older, and dispensing advice during difficult stages of their lives. (3)

Though there's no formal arrangement to their godparent relationship, in many ways, Scott and Hoffman are fulfilling the role of *co-parents*, a concept that's been gaining popularity around the world. In a co-parenting arrangement, the biological parent or parents of a child ask close friends or relatives to assist in the care and nurturing of their children. It's like the role of a favorite aunt or uncle, only slightly more formal and adapted to the complications of modern life. (4)

In truth, co-parenting is an old concept with a new name. According to the London-based Institute for Social Inventions' publication *The Book of Visions*, the tradition of asking close friends or family to play a key role in a child's upbringing goes back to the fourth century. There are even words for people who play such a role, *commater* and *compater*, that can be traced to the end of the sixth century. (5)

For couples like Hoffman and Scott who have chosen not to have children of their own, co-parenting is a way to welcome kids into their lives—without letting their lives be taken over by children. (6)

"When the girls were little, we could take the girls for the weekend, whenever we wanted a kid fix," Scott says. "They were so much fun." But did building such a close relationship make Scott regret not having children of her own? "No," she answers firmly. "In fact, it made me really happy with my decision not to be a parent. I saw firsthand how demanding it is to be a parent and how little I wanted that to be my full-time responsibility." (7)

For single parents, two-career families, or couples living away from their immediate families, co-parents can be a godsend. Holly Coughlin, a Minneapolis-based graphic designer, spends time each week with Chantz, the 9-year-old son of her ex-partner. Though she's no longer in contact with Chantz's father, Coughlin has remained friends with his ex-wife, and the two women continue to share time with the boy, attending his school conferences and getting together for dinner. (8)

Chantz's mother has not remarried, so Coughlin's help is doubly appreciated. "Sometimes when she is going out of town she needs me to stay with him. I always tell her I'd do that in a minute," says Coughlin, who has no children of her own. "Chantz's mother always tells him, 'You can never have too many people who love you,' and it's true. I love him so much and I want him to know that." (9)

When Coughlin, who is of Korean heritage, and Chantz, whose father is Filipino American, are out in public, people often mistake them for mother and son. "It's silly," Coughlin says, "because if you really look at us we don't look anything alike except for the color of our skin. In fact, Chantz looks just like his mother." Still, because the mistake is made so often, the pair have had to come up with a word to describe their relationship to others. *Co-parent* sounds too formal. (10)

"So we use *ate* (pronounced AH-tay), the Filipino word for older woman who is not related by blood but who cares for you," Coughlin explains. "I call him *ading*, which means a younger person who is not my son, but a younger close friend. If we want to keep the explanations short, we just say, 'This is my friend,' because we are friends—we just happen to be different ages." (11)

Some suggest making the co-parent relationship more official, perhaps through a ceremony similar to the one held for godparents at baptisms. In *The Book of Visions*, Angela Murphy of London suggests that "parents . . . choose people with whom they [wish] to create a formal state of friendship (just as in rites of blood-brotherhood). Now that extended family is stretched and scattered, it is even more important to confirm bonds of friendship." (12)

So maybe a ceremony is in order to invest the co-parenting relationship with its proper significance. Or maybe, as Scott and Hoffman can attest, a relationship that begins with a promise to a pair of expectant parents can, over the years, assume a life of its own. (13)

"I'm really happy that we have the identity of godmothers," Scott says. "It elevates us a notch above *friend of the family*. For me, there's tremendous joy in having these kids in my life over the long haul. They know we're happy for them, and that makes me really happy." (14)

EXPLORING VOCABULARY

Define the words *commater* and *compater*. You may want to begin by examining and defining the prefix *com* (see page 203) and then looking up each word root. From what language do the roots come?

EXPLORING THE TEXT

1. How many people does Steiner interview?
2. Steiner interviews the co-parents only. Why did he not include interviews with the parents and their children? How would this article be different if he had?

3. What sources—other than interviews—does Steiner bring into the article? (Review your annotations.)
4. What is the purpose of this article?

EXPLORING ISSUES AND IDEAS

1. Would you like to be a co-parent or recruit co-parents for your children? Why?
2. What benefits do the co-parents receive from being co-parents? What responsibilities do they hold?
3. How do the children benefit by having co-parents?
4. What is it about modern American life that makes the idea of co-parenting attractive to parents?
5. Is there anyone in your life that you think of as a co-parent?

SUGGESTIONS FOR READING BOOKS ABOUT PHENOMENA

Men Are From Mars, Women Are From Venus by John Gray, Ph.D.

Jurassic Park by Michael Crichton

Into the Wild by Jon Krakauer

SUGGESTIONS FOR SUMMARIZING ESSAYS ABOUT PHENOMENA

Choose one of the following works from Unit Four and write a summary. Follow the guidelines for writing a summary on page 207.

"Now Hear This: Shhhhhhhhhh" by Jeanette Batz

"Hooked on Anger" by Russell Baker

SUGGESTIONS FOR WRITING ABOUT PHENOMENA

1. Choose a phenomenon in your community, neighborhood, school, family, etc. and write an essay that describes and explains the phenomenon. Use the profile sheet in this unit to help you gather information.

2. Write a letter to Toufexis and share with her your own ideas about romantic love. Be sure to include a strong controlling idea.

3. Write a letter to Baker and share with him your ideas about why Americans are so angry. Be sure to include a strong controlling idea.

4. Write an essay in which you define the word *phenomenon* and then support your definition with specific examples. You may want to use the phenomena written about in this unit as support for your definition and/or you may want to use your own experiences.

5. Read one of the books listed and write an essay profiling the phenomenon it discusses. Use the profile sheet in this unit to help you gather information.

6. Write an essay in which you contrast your explanation of a phenomenon with an explanation offered by one of the authors in this unit.

7. Write a newspaper article reporting the phenomenon described in "The Tell-Tale Heart." Use the profile sheet to gather information before writing your essay.

PROFILING PHENOMENA

A phenomenon is something extraordinary or remarkable that can be observed; it is exceptional or notable. Fill in the following information about one or more of the phenomena you have read about in Unit Four. Remember that the information in some categories may not be directly stated; it may be implied. If it is implied, use clues given by the author to infer the answer. Remember also that the information in some categories may not be directly stated or implied, so do not just guess at any given category.

DESCRIPTION _____

PURPOSE/FUNCTION _____

LOCATION _____

CAUSE/ORIGIN _____

DISTINGUISHING CHARACTERISTICS _____

PARTICIPANTS _____

NUMBER _____

NAME(S) _____

AGE(S) _____

SOCIOECONOMIC LEVEL(S) _____

CULTURAL/PHILOSOPHICAL AFFILIATION(S) _____

REACTIONS OF PARTICIPANTS _____

CONSEQUENCES TO PARTICIPANTS _____

CONSEQUENCES TO ENVIRONMENT _____

UNIT V

ISSUES

What Is Poverty? (Speech)

Jo Goodwin Parker

PREREADING

In a free write, answer the question presented in the title of this selection.

ANNOTATING

While reading, underline any words, phrases, or sentences that make you feel uncomfortable. In the margins, briefly note why you feel uncomfortable.

You ask me what is poverty? Listen to me. Here I am, dirty, smelly, and with no "proper" underwear on and with the stench of my rotting teeth near you. I will tell you. Listen to me. Listen without pity. I cannot use your pity. Listen with understanding. Put yourself in my dirty, worn out, ill-fitting shoes and hear me.   (1)

Poverty is getting up every morning from a dirt- and illness-stained mattress. The sheets have long since been used for diapers. Poverty is living in a smell that never leaves. This is a smell of urine, sour milk, and spoiling food sometimes joined with the strong smell of long-cooked onions. Onions are cheap. If you have smelled this smell, you did not know how it came. It is the smell of the outdoor privy. It is the smell of young children who cannot walk the long dark way in the night. It is the smell of the mattresses where years of "accidents" have happened. It is the smell of the milk which has gone sour because the refrigerator long has not worked, and it costs money to get fixed. It is the smell of rotting garbage. I could bury it, but where is the shovel? Shovels cost money.   (2)

Poverty is being tired. I have always been tired. They told me at the hospital when the last baby came that I had chronic anemia caused from poor diet, a bad case of worms, and that I needed a corrective operation. I listened politely—the poor are always polite. The poor always listen. They don't say that there is no money for iron pills, or better food, or worm medicine. The idea of an operation is frightening and costs so much that, if I had dared, I would have laughed. Who takes care of my children? Recovery from an operation takes a long time. I have three children. When I left them with "Granny" the last time I had a job, I came home to find the baby covered with fly specks and a diaper that had not been changed since I left. When the dried diaper came off, bits of my baby's flesh came with it. My other child was playing with a sharp bit of broken glass, and my oldest was playing alone at the edge of the lake. I made twenty-two dollars a week, and a good nursery school costs twenty dollars a week for three children. I quit my job.   (3)

Poverty is dirt. You say in your clean clothes coming from your clean house, "anybody can be clean." Let me explain about housekeeping with no money. For breakfast, I give my children grits with no oleo or cornbread without eggs and oleo. This does not use up many dishes. What dishes there are, I wash in cold water and with no soap. Even the cheapest soap has to be saved for the baby's diapers. Look at my hands, so cracked and red. Once I saved for two months to buy a jar of Vaseline for my hands and the baby's diaper rash. When I had saved enough, I went to buy it and the price had gone up two cents. The baby and I suffered on. I have to decide every day if I can bear to put my cracked, sore hands into the cold water and strong soap. But you ask, why not hot water? Fuel costs money. If you have a wood fire it costs money. If you burn electricity, it costs money. Hot water is a luxury. I do not have luxuries. I know you will be surprised when I tell you how young I am. I look so much older. My back has been bent over the wash tubs for so long, I cannot remember when I did anything else. Every night I wash every stitch my school age child has on and just hope her clothes will be dry by morning.   (4)

Poverty is staying up all night on cold nights to watch the fire, knowing one spark on the newspaper covering the walls means your sleeping children die in flames. In summer poverty is watching gnats and flies devour your baby's tears when he cries. The screens are torn and you pay so little rent you know they will never be fixed. Poverty means insects in your food, in your nose, in your eyes, and crawling over you when you sleep. Poverty is hoping it never rains because diapers won't dry when it rains and soon you are using newspapers. Poverty is seeing your children forever with runny noses. Paper handkerchiefs cost money and all your rags you need for other things. Even more costly are antihistamines. Poverty is cooking without food and cleaning without soap. (5)

Poverty is asking for help. Have you ever had to ask for help, knowing your children will suffer unless you get it? Think about asking for a loan from a relative, if this is the only way you can imagine asking for help. I will tell you how it feels. You find out where the office is that you are supposed to visit. You circle that block four or five times. Thinking of your children, you go in. Everyone is busy. Finally, someone comes out and you tell her that you need help. That never is the person you need to see. You go see another person, and after spilling the whole shame of your poverty all over the desk between you, you find that this isn't the right office after all—you must repeat the whole process, and it never is any easier at the next place. (6)

You have asked for help, and after all it has a cost. You are again told to wait. You are told why, but you don't really hear because of the red cloud of shame and the rising black cloud of despair. (7)

Poverty is remembering. It is remembering quitting school in junior high because "nice" children had been so cruel about my clothes and my smell. The attendance officer came. My mother told him I was pregnant. I wasn't but she thought that I could get a job and help out. I had jobs off and on, but never long enough to learn anything. Mostly I remember being married. I was so young then. I am still young. For a time, we had all the things you have. There was a little house in another town, with hot water and everything. Then my husband lost his job. There was unemployment insurance for a while and what few jobs I could get. Soon, all our nice things were repossessed and we moved back here. I was pregnant then. This house didn't look so bad when we first moved in. Every week it gets worse. Nothing is ever fixed. We now had no money. There were a few odd jobs for my husband, but everything went for food then, as it does now. I don't know how we lived through three years and three babies, but we did. I'll tell you something, after the last baby I destroyed my marriage. It had been a good one, but could you keep bringing children into this dirt? Did you ever think how much it costs for any kind of birth control? I knew my husband was leaving the day he left, but there were no good-byes between us. I hope he has been able to climb out of this mess somewhere. He never could hope with us to drag him down. (8)

That's when I asked for help. When I got it, you know how much it was? It was, and is, seventy-eight dollars a month for the four of us; that is all I can ever get. Now you know why there is no soap, no needles and thread, no hot water, no aspirin, no worm medicine, no hand cream, no shampoo. None of these things forever and ever and ever. So that you can see clearly, I pay twenty dollars a month rent, and most of the rest goes for food. For grits and cornmeal, and rice and milk and beans. I try my best to use only the minimum electricity. If I use more, there is that much less for food. (9)

Poverty is looking into a black future. Your children won't play with my boys. They will turn to other boys who steal to get what they want. I can already see them behind the bars of their prison instead of the bars of my poverty. Or they will turn to the freedom of alcohol or drugs, and find themselves enslaved. And my daughter? At best, there is for her a life like mine. (10)

But you say to me, there are schools. Yes, there are schools. My children have no extra books, no magazines, no extra pencils, or crayons, or paper and the most important of all, they do not have health. They have worms, they have infections, they have pinkeye all summer. They do not sleep well on the floor, or with me in my one bed. They do not suffer from hunger, my seventy-eight dollars keeps us alive, but they do suffer from malnutrition. Oh yes, I do remember what I was taught about health in school. It doesn't do much good. In some places there is a surplus commodities program. Not here. The county said it cost too much. There is a school lunch program. But I have two children who will already be damaged by the time they get to school. (11)

But, you say to me, there are health clinics. Yes, there are health clinics and they are in the towns. I live out here eight miles from town. I can walk that far (even if it is sixteen miles both ways), but can my little children? My neighbor will take me when he goes; but he expects to get paid, *one way or another*. I bet you know my neighbor. He is that large man who spends his time at the gas station, the

barbershop, and the corner store complaining about the government
spending money on the immoral mothers of illegitimate children.   (12)

Poverty is an acid that drips on pride until all pride is worn away.
Poverty is a chisel that chips on honor until honor is worn away. Some
of you say that you would do *something* in my situation, and maybe you
would, for the first week or the first month, but for year after year after
year?   (13)

Even the poor can dream. A dream of time when there is money.
Money for the right kinds of food, for worm medicine, for iron pills,
for toothbrushes, for hand cream, for a hammer and nails and a bit of
screening, for a shovel, for a bit of paint, for some sheeting, for needles
and thread. Money to pay *in money* for a trip to town. And, oh, money
for hot water and money for soap. A dream of when asking for help
does not eat away the last bit of pride. When the office you visit is as
nice as the offices of other governmental agencies, when there are
enough workers to help you quickly, when workers do not quit in
defeat and despair. When you have to tell your story to only one
person, and that person can send you for other help and you don't
have to prove your poverty over and over and over again.   (14)

I have come out of my despair to tell you this. Remember I did not
come from another place or another time. Others like me are all
around you. Look at us with an angry heart, anger that will help you
help me. Anger that will let you tell of me. The poor are always silent.
Can you be silent too?   (15)

EXPLORING VOCABULARY

With a small group of your classmates, make a list of as many adjectives
as possible to describe poverty from Parker's point of view. Try not to
use the adjectives she uses; come up with your own.

PROFILING ISSUES

Using the profile sheet on page 198, write a profile of the issue Parker
describes. You may have to read between the lines—or make inferences—to address some of the categories. When you are finished, discuss
your answers with a small group of your peers or with the entire class.

EXPLORING THE TEXT

1. How does Parker organize her speech? Is this organization effective?
2. How is this speech similar to an essay? How is it different?
3. What is Parker's main idea?
4. What is her tone?

EXPLORING IDEAS

1. Does Parker's speech make you feel uncomfortable? Why? (Review your annotations.)
2. What is Parker's view of the agencies that are supposed to help those in poverty? Why?
3. Do you think Parker's experience of poverty is typical?
4. In paragraph fourteen, Parker writes, "Even the poor can dream." What does she dream about? How are her dreams different than your dreams?
5. What does Parker mean in the last paragraph when she asks, "Can you be silent too?"

A Valuable Tapestry (RADIO BROADCAST)

SHIRLEY HART BERRY

PREREADING

America is often called the great "melting pot." Do some research and find out what that term means and when it originated. Share your findings with the class.

ANNOTATING

While reading, underline any idea with which you strongly agree or strongly disagree. In the margins, briefly note why.

In my family is a quilt that my grandmother made. It's a beautiful quilt. Do you know what makes the quilt so wonderful? Yes, it has warmth. And the size is a good one. But its beauty lies in the pieces that make it complete. Some of the pieces are corduroy; some, satin; others, wool or gabardine. The colors are dark, pastel, flowered, striped. A rich variety of color, pattern, and texture. Now would this quilt be a good one if all pieces were the same? Obviously, it would cover us; it would keep us warm; but a quilt of fabric made from dresses from my childhood, a square from an old coat, a piece of a wedding dress, the pocket of an apron . . . each piece has its own story and together they make a patchwork of wonder and delight.   (1)

So it is with this nation. True, we could all talk the same, worship the same, have the same attitudes, but how much more wonderful that we, like the pieces of my quilt, have our own story, that our differences give our stories; hence, our country—so much more wonder and delight.   (2)

Those differences, then,—that diversity—is what we draw attention to when some of us use a label of a compound word: Spanish American, Japanese American, Irish American.   (3)

What does it mean to be a compound? By *compound* I mean what some people call a "hyphenated American." Does it mean that one's emphasis is on the part that comes before the hyphen? That is, if one is Italian American, does that mean that she has more allegiance to Italy than to the United States? Of course not. When one calls herself an Italian American, she proclaims her native heritage while still participating in the precepts of this nation. To be an Italian American makes one no less an American.   (4)

Yes, those of us who use a compound term accept this American culture. The American culture is the system that we have in common. Asian American, European American, African American—each compound ends with the word *American*. That we are all American allows us to share this democracy, a language, our own pursuits to happiness. This American culture, however, came about because of a combination of many other cultures, customs, and traditions. How much better we are as a people, an American people, that we have room for such variety. We feel proud to see the American flag. We cheer when our troops go marching in. We vote. We pay taxes. We teach our children to respect authority. And we do one more thing. We appreciate the value that all of us bring to this American culture.   (5)

But let's clear up this idea of hyphenation. We are NOT hyphenated Americans. To be Polish American, to be African American, or to be from any other nation or continent combined with the word American—a derivation of the United States of America—is not to be hyphenated. When you write the words, omit the hyphen. When you say the words, don't think hyphen. When you think the term, no hyphen. Instead, think COMPOUND; think COMBINATION; think ACCEPTANCE of all the wonderful people who came here or who were brought here or who were already here. Think APPRECIATION for the diversity that gives this nation wonder and delight.   (6)

To ask people to stop saying that they are Mexican American or Swedish American is to refuse to realize that our diversity IS the uniqueness of the United States. Just as Grandmother's quilt shows family history through its variety of fabrics, we are reminded of our nation's history through the words we call ourselves. Stop being African American? I can no more not be an African American than I can not be a woman. I'm proud of my heritage. I also appreciate the contributions of other compound Americans that make these United States the valuable tapestry we are.

(7)

EXPLORING VOCABULARY

Look up the word *compound* in the dictionary. Then, using a thesaurus, see if there are any other words that could be used to describe compound Americans.

PROFILING ISSUES

Using the profile sheet on page 198, write a profile of the issue Berry describes. You may have to read between the lines—or make inferences—to address some of the categories. When you are finished, discuss your answers with a small group of your peers or with the entire class.

EXPLORING THE TEXT

1. What is Berry's main idea?
2. What is her tone?
3. How might this work be different if it were an essay or a newspaper article?

EXPLORING IDEAS

1. How does Berry's description of America as a quilt differ from others' description of America as a melting pot?
2. According to Berry, what unites Americans?
3. Overall, do you agree with Berry? Why or why not? (Review your annotations.)
4. Are you a "compound American"?

In Praise of the F Word (Essay)

MARY SHERRY

PREREADING

Free write about a time you failed at doing something—taking a test, passing a course, or accomplishing a goal. How did failing make you feel? How did failing affect your behavior in future projects?

ANNOTATING

While reading, underline Sherry's points. In the margins, note whether you agree or disagree with her.

Tens of thousands of 18-year-olds will graduate this year and be handed meaningless diplomas. These diplomas won't look any different from those awarded their luckier classmates. Their validity will be questioned only when their employers discover that these graduates are semiliterate. (1)

Eventually a fortunate few will find their way into educational-repair shops—adult-literacy programs, such as the one where I teach basic grammar and writing. There, high-school graduates and high-school dropouts pursuing graduate-equivalency certificates will learn the skills they should have learned in school. They will also discover they have been cheated by our educational system. (2)

As I teach, I learn a lot about our schools. Early in each session I ask my students to write about an unpleasant experience they had in school. No writers' block here! "I wish someone would have made me stop doing drugs and made me study." "I liked to party and no one seemed to care." "I was a good kid and didn't cause any trouble, so they just passed me along even though I didn't read well and couldn't write." And so on. (3)

I am your basic do-gooder, and prior to teaching this class, I blamed the poor academic skills our kids have today on drugs, divorce, and other impediments to concentration necessary for doing well in school. But, as I rediscover each time I walk into the classroom, before a teacher can expect students to concentrate, he has to get their attention, no matter what distractions may be at hand. There are many ways to do this, and they have much to do with teaching style. However, if style alone won't do it, there is another way to show who holds the winning hand in the classroom. That is to reveal the trump card of failure.   (4)

I will never forget a teacher who played that card to get the attention of one of my children. Our youngest, a world-class charmer, did little to develop his intellectual talents but always got by. Until Mrs. Stifter.   (5)

Our son was a high-school senior when he had her for English. "He sits in the back of the room talking to his friends," she told me. "Why don't you move him to the front row?" I urged, believing the embarrassment would get him to settle down. Mrs. Stifter looked at me steely-eyed over her glasses. "I don't move seniors," she said. "I flunk them." I was flustered. Our son's academic life flashed before my eyes. No teacher had ever threatened him with that before. I regained my composure and managed to say that I thought she was right. By the time I got home I was feeling pretty good about this. It was a radical approach for these times, but, well, why not? "She's going to flunk you," I told my son. I did not discuss it any further. Suddenly English became a priority in his life. He finished out the semester with an A.   (6)

I know one example doesn't make a case, but at night I see a parade of students who are angry and resentful for having been passed along until they could no longer even pretend to keep up. Of average intelligence or better, they eventually quit school, concluding they were too dumb to finish. "I should have been held back" is a comment I hear frequently. Even sadder are those students who are high-school graduates who say to me after a few weeks of class, "I don't know how I ever got a high-school diploma."   (7)

Passing students who have not mastered the work cheats them and the employers who expect graduates to have basic skills. We excuse this dishonest behavior by saying kids can't learn if they come from terrible environments. No one stops to think that—no matter what environments they come from—most kids don't put school first on their list unless they perceive something is at stake. They'd rather be sailing. (8)

Many students I see at night could give expert testimony on unemployment, chemical dependency, abusive relationships. In spite of these difficulties, they have decided to make education a priority. They are motivated by the desire for a better job or the need to hang on to the one they've got. They have a healthy fear of failure. (9)

People of all ages can rise above their problems, but they need to have a reason to do so. Young people generally don't have the maturity to value education in the same way my adult students value it. But fear of failure, whether economic or academic, can motivate both. (10)

Flunking as a regular policy has just as much merit today as it did two generations ago. We must review the threat of flunking and see it as it really is—a positive teaching tool. It is an expression of confidence by both teachers and parents that the students have the ability to learn the material presented to them. However, making it work again would take a dedicated, caring conspiracy between teachers and parents. It would mean facing the tough reality that passing kids who haven't learned the material—while it might save them grief for the short term—dooms them to long-term illiteracy. It would mean that teachers would have to follow through on their threats, and parents would have to stand behind them, knowing their children's best interests are indeed at stake. This means no more doing Scott's assignments for him because he might fail. No more passing Jodi because she's such a nice kid. (11)

This is a policy that worked in the past and can work today. A wise teacher, with the support of his parents, gave our son the opportunity to succeed—or fail. It's time we return this choice to all students. (12)

EXPLORING VOCABULARY

In paragraph two, Sherry uses the term *educational-repair shop*. What does she mean?

PROFILING ISSUES

Using the profile sheet on page 198, write a profile of the issue Sherry describes. You may have to read between the lines—or make inferences—

to address some of the categories. When you are finished, discuss your answers with a small group of your peers or with the entire class.

EXPLORING THE TEXT

1. What is Sherry's main point?
2. What kind of evidence does she use to support her point?
3. Who is her intended audience?
4. What is the purpose of her essay?

EXPLORING IDEAS

1. In paragraph seven, Sherry writes, " 'I should have been held back' is a comment I frequently hear." Is that a comment you frequently hear or have heard from classmates?
2. Do you agree with Sherry's main point and her supporting points? Why or why not? (Review your annotations.)
3. Are there any alternate ways to motivate students to take their schoolwork more seriously? What are they?
4. According to Sherry, why don't teachers fail students more often?

The Hammer Man (SHORT STORY)

TONI CADE BAMBARA

PREREADING

Free write about someone in your life with whom you have or had an adversarial relationship. Consider why you do not get along with this person. Also consider what you would do if someone else tried to hurt this person. Share your ideas with the class.

ANNOTATING

While reading, underline any words, phrases, or sentences that express the narrator's feelings about the character named Manny. In the margins, write a word that describes the narrator's feelings.

I was glad to hear that Manny had fallen off the roof. I had put out the tale that I was down with yellow fever, but nobody paid me no mind, least of all Dirty Red who stomped right in to announce that Manny had fallen off the roof and that I could come out of hiding now. My mother dropped what she was doing, which was the laundry, and got the whole story out of Red. "Bad enough you gots to hang around with boys," she said. "But fight with them too. And you would pick the craziest one at that."

(1)

Manny was supposed to be crazy. That was his story. To say you were bad put some people off. But to say you were crazy, well, you were officially not to be messed with. So that was his story. On the other hand, after I called him what I called him and said a few choice things about his mother, his face did go through some piercing changes. And I did kind of wonder if maybe he sure was nuts. I didn't wait to find out. I got in the wind. And then he waited for me on my stoop all day and all night, not hardly speaking to the people going in and out. And he was there all day Saturday, with his sister bringing him peanut-butter sandwiches and cream sodas. He must've gone to the bathroom right there cause every time I looked out the kitchen window, there he was. And Sunday, too. I got to thinking the boy was mad. (2)

"You got no sense of humor, that's your trouble," I told him. He looked up, but he didn't say nothing. All at once I was real sorry about the whole thing. I should've settled for hitting off the little girls in the school yard, or waiting for Frankie to come in so we could raise some kind of hell. This way, I had to play sick when my mother was around cause my father had already taken away my BB gun and hid it. (3)

I don't know how they got Manny on the roof finally. Maybe the Wakefield kids, the ones who keep the pigeons, called him up. Manny was a sucker for sick animals and things like that. Or maybe Frankie got some nasty girls to go up on the roof with him and got Manny to join him. I don't know. Anyway, the catwalk had lost all its cement and the roof always did kind of slant downward. So Manny fell off the roof. I got over my yellow fever right quick, needless to say, and ventured outside. But by this time I had already told Miss Rose that Crazy Manny was after me. And Miss Rose, being who she was, quite naturally went over to Manny's house and said a few harsh words to his mother, who, being who she was, chased Miss Rose out into the street and they commenced to get with it, snatching bottles out of the garbage cans and breaking them on the Johnny pumps and stuff like that. (4)

Dirty Red didn't have to tell us about this. Everybody could see and hear all. I never figured the garbage cans for an arsenal, but Miss Rose came up with sticks and table legs and things, and Manny's mother had her share of scissor blades and bicycle chains. They got to rolling in the streets and all you could see was pink drawers and fat legs. It was something else. Miss Rose is nutty but Manny's mother's crazier than Manny. They were at it a couple of times during my sick spell. Everyone would congregate on the window sills or the fire escape, commenting that it was still much too cold for this kind of nonsense. But they watched anyway. And then Manny fell off the roof. And that was that. Miss Rose went back to her dream books and Manny's mother went back to her tumbled-down kitchen of dirty clothes and bundles and bundles of rags and children. (5)

My father got in on it too, cause he happened to ask Manny one night why he was sitting on the stoop like that every night. Manny told him right off that he was going to kill me the first chance he got. Quite naturally this made my father a little warm, me being his only daughter and planning to become a doctor and take care of him in his old age. So he had a few words with Manny first, and then he got hold of the older brother, Bernard, who was more his size. Bernard didn't see how any of it was his business or my father's business, so my father got mad and jammed Bernard's head into the mailbox. Then my father started getting messages from Bernard's uncle about where to meet him for a showdown and all. My father didn't say a word to my mother all this time; just sat around mumbling and picking up the phone and putting it down, or grabbing my stickball bat and putting it back. He carried on like this for days till I thought I would scream if the yellow fever didn't have me so weak. And then Manny fell off the roof, and my father went back to his beer-drinking buddies.   (6)

I was in the school yard, pitching pennies with the little boys from the elementary school, when my friend Violet hits my brand-new Spaudeen over the wall. She came running back to tell me that Manny was coming down the block. I peeked beyond the fence and there he was alright. He had his head all wound up like a mummy and his arm in a sling and his leg in a cast. It looked phony to me, especially that walking cane. I figured Dirty Red had told me a tale just to get me out there so Manny could stomp me, and Manny was playing it up with costume and all till he could get me.   (7)

"What happened to him?" Violet's sisters whispered. But I was too busy trying to figure out how this act was supposed to work. Then Manny passed real close to the fence and gave me a look.   (8)

"You had enough, Hammer Head," I yelled. "Just bring your crummy self in this yard and I'll pick up where I left off." Violet was knocked out and the other kids went into a huddle. I didn't have to say anything else. And when they all pressed me later, I just said, "You know that hammer he always carries in his fatigues?" And they'd all nod waiting for the rest of a long story. "Well, I took it away from him." And I walked off nonchalantly.   (9)

Manny stayed indoors for a long time. I almost forgot about him. New kids moved into the block and I got all caught up with that. And then Miss Rose finally hit the numbers and started ordering a whole lot of stuff through the mail and we would sit on the curb and watch these weird-looking packages being carried in, trying to figure out what simpleminded thing she had thrown her money away on when she might just as well wait for the warm weather and throw a block party for all her godchildren. (10)

After a while a center opened up and my mother said she'd increase my allowance if I went and joined because I'd have to get out of my pants and stay in skirts, on account of that's the way things were at the center. So I joined and got to thinking about everything else but old Hammer Head. It was a rough place to get along in, the center, but my mother said that I needed to be be'd with and she needed to not be with me, so I went. And that time I sneaked into the office, that's when I really got turned on. I looked into one of those not-quite-white folders and saw that I was from a deviant family in a deviant neighborhood. I showed my mother the word in the dictionary, but she didn't pay me no mind. It was my favorite word after that. I ran it into the ground till one day my father got the strap just to show how deviant he could get. So I gave up trying to improve my vocabulary. And I almost gave up my dungarees. (11)

Then one night, I'm walking past the Douglas Street park cause I got thrown out of the center for playing pool when I should've been sewing, even though I had already decided that this was going to be my last fling with boy things, and starting tomorrow I was going to fix my hair right and wear skirts all the time just so my mother would stop talking about her gray hairs, and Miss Rose would stop calling me by my brother's name by mistake. So I'm walking past the park and there's ole Manny on the basketball court, perfecting his lay-ups and talking with himself. Being me, I quite naturally walk right up and ask what the hell he's doing playing in the dark, and he looks up and all around like the dark had crept up on him when he wasn't looking. So I knew right away that he'd been out there for a long time with his eyes just going along with the program. (12)

"There was two seconds to go and we were one point behind," he said, shaking his head and staring at his sneakers like they was somebody. "And I was in the clear. I'd left the man in the backcourt and there I was, smiling, you dig, cause it was in the bag. They passed the ball and I slid the ball up nice and easy cause there was nothing to worry about. And . . ." He shook his head. "I muffed the goddamn shot. Ball bounced off the rim . . ." He stared at his hands. "The game of the season. Last game." And then he ignored me altogether, though he wasn't talking to me in the first place. He went back to his lay-ups, always from the same spot with his arms crooked in the same way, over and over. I must've gotten hypnotized cause I probably stood there for at least an hour watching like a fool till I couldn't even see the damn ball, much less the basket. But I stood there anyway for no reason I know of. He never missed. But he cursed himself away. It was torture. And then a squad car pulled up and a short cop with hair like one of the Marx Brothers came out hitching up his pants. He looked real hard at me and then at Manny.   (13)

"What are you two doing?"   (14)

"He's doing a lay-up. I'm watching," I said with my smart self.   (15)

Then the cop just stood there and finally turned to the other one who was just getting out of the car.   (16)

"Who unlocked the gate?" the big one said.   (17)

"It's always unlocked," I said. Then we three just stood there like a bunch of penguins watching Manny go at it.   (18)

"This on the level?" the big guy asked, tilting his hat back with the thumb the way big guys do in hot weather. "Hey, you," he said, walking over to Manny. "I'm talking to you." He finally grabbed the ball to get Manny's attention. But that didn't work. Manny just stood there with his arms out waiting for the pass so he could save the game. He wasn't paying no mind to the cop. So, quite naturally, when the cop slapped him upside his head it was a surprise. And when the cop started counting three to go, Manny had already recovered from the slap and was just ticking off the seconds before the buzzer sounded and all was lost.   (19)

"Gimme the ball, man." Manny's face was all tightened up and ready to pop.   (20)

"Did you hear what I said, black boy?"   (21)

Now, when somebody says that word like that, I gets warm. And crazy or no crazy, Manny was my brother at that moment and the cop was the enemy.   (22)

"You better give him back his ball," I said. "Manny don't take no mess from no cops. He ain't bothering nobody. He's gonna be Mister Basketball when he grows up. Just trying to get a little practice in before the softball season starts."   (23)

"Look here, sister, we'll run you in too," Harpo said.   (24)

"I damn sure can't be your sister seeing how I'm a black girl. Boy, I sure will be glad when you run me in so I can tell everybody about that. You must think you're in the South, mister."   (25)

The big guy screwed his mouth up and let one of them hard-day sighs. "The park's closed, little girl, so why don't you and your boyfriend go on home."   (26)

That really got me. The "little girl" was bad enough but that "boyfriend" was too much. But I kept cool, mostly because Manny looked so pitiful waiting there with his hands in a time-out and there being no one to stop the clock. But I kept my cool mostly cause of that hammer in Manny's pocket and no telling how frantic things can get with a big mouth like me, a couple of wise cops and a crazy boy too.   (27)

"The gates are open," I said real quiet-like, "and this here's a free country. So why don't you give him back his ball?"   (28)

The big cop did another one of those sighs, his specialty I guess, and then he bounced the ball to Manny who went right into his gliding thing clear up to the blackboard, damn near like he was some kind of very beautiful bird. And then he swooshed that ball in, even if there was no net, and you couldn't really hear the swoosh. Something happened to the bones in my chest. It was something.   (29)

"Crazy kids anyhow," the one with the wig said and turned to go. But the big guy watched Manny for a while and I guess something must've snapped in his head, cause all of a sudden he was hot for taking Manny to jail or court or somewhere and started yelling at him and everything, which is a bad thing to do to Manny, I can tell you. And I'm standing there thinking that none of my teachers, from kindergarten right on up, none of them knew what they were talking about. I'll be damned if I ever knew one of them rosy-cheeked cops that smiled and helped you get to school without neither you or your little raggedy dog getting hit by a truck that had a smile on its face, too. Not that I ever believed it. I knew Dick and Jane was full of crap from the get-go, especially them cops. Like this dude, for example, pulling on Manny's clothes like that when obviously he had just done about the most beautiful thing a man can do and not be a fag. No cop could swoosh without a net.   (30)

"Look out, man," was all Manny said, but it was the way he pushed the cop that started the real yelling and threats. And I thought to myself, Oh God here I am trying to change my ways, and not talk back in school, and do like my mother wants, but just have this last fling, and now this—getting shot in the stomach and bleeding to death in Douglas Street park and poor Manny getting pistol-whipped by those bastards and whatnot. I could see it all, practically crying too. And it just wasn't no kind of thing to happen to a small child like me with my confirmation picture in the paper next to my weeping parents and schoolmates. I could feel the blood sticking to my shirt and my eyeballs slipping away, and then that confirmation picture again; and my mother and her gray hair; and Miss Rose heading for the precinct with a shotgun; and my father getting old and feeble with no one to doctor him up and all.   (31)

And I wished Manny had fallen off the damn roof and died right then and there and saved me all this aggravation of being killed with him by these cops who surely didn't come out of no fifth-grade reader. But it didn't happen. They just took the ball and Manny followed them real quiet-like right out of the park into the dark, into the squad car with his head drooping and his arms in a crook. And I went on home cause what the hell am I going to do on a basketball court, and it getting to be nearly midnight?   (32)

I didn't see Manny no more after he got into that squad car. But they didn't kill him after all cause Miss Rose heard he was in some kind of big house for people who lose their marbles. And then it was spring finally, and me and Violet was in this very boss fashion show at the center. And Miss Rose bought me my first corsage—yellow roses to match my shoes.   (33)

EXPLORING VOCABULARY

Look up the word *deviant* in the dictionary. Then reread paragraph eleven and explain why the narrator got so upset when the word was used to describe her family.

PROFILING ISSUES

Using the profile sheet on page 198, write a profile of one of the issues the narrator describes. You may have to read between the lines—or make inferences—to address some of the categories. When you are finished, discuss your answers with a small group of your peers or with the entire class.

EXPLORING THE TEXT

1. What is the theme of the story?
2. How might this story be different if it were told from Manny's point of view?
3. What is the significance of the title?
4. What is the narrator's tone?

EXPLORING IDEAS

1. What is the nature of the relationship between Manny and the narrator?
2. Why does the narrator stand up for Manny?
3. What social issues are addressed in this story?
4. Why did the police take Manny to jail?
5. Do you know someone who was mistreated by the police? What happened?

The Powwow at the End of the World (POEM)

SHERMAN ALEXIE

PREREADING

Look at a map of the Northwestern part of the United States and find the Grand Coulee Dam, the Columbia River, and the Spokane River. Find, also, the names of the Native American tribes who inhabit(ed) that area of the country.

ANNOTATING

While reading, place a slash (/) at the end of each sentence. In the margins, write out what you think each sentence means.

I am told by many of you that I must forgive and so I shall
after an Indian woman puts her shoulder to the Grand Coulee Dam
and topples it. I am told by many of you that I must forgive
and so I shall after the floodwaters burst each successive dam
downriver from the Grand Coulee. I am told by many of you   (5)
that I must forgive and so I shall after the floodwaters find
their way to the mouth of the Columbia River as it enters the Pacific
and causes all of it to rise. I am told by many of you that I must forgive
and so I shall after the first drop of floodwater is swallowed by that
    salmon
waiting in the Pacific. I am told by many of you that I must forgive   (10)
    and so I shall
after that salmon swims upstream, through the mouth of the Columbia
and then past the flooded cities, broken dams and abandoned reactors
of Hanford. I am told by many of you that I must forgive and so I shall   (15)

after that salmon swims through the mouth of the Spokane River
as it meets the Columbia, then upstream, until it arrives
in the shallow of a secret bay on the reservation where I wait alone.
I am told by many of you that I must forgive and so I shall after
that salmon leaps into the night air above the water, throws   (20)
a lightning bolt at the brush near my feet and starts the fire
which will lead all of the Indians home. I am told
by many of you that I must forgive and so I shall
after we Indians have gathered around the fire with that salmon
who has three stories it must tell before sunrise: one story will teach us   (25)
how to pray; another story will make us laugh for hours;
the third story will give us reason to dance. I am told by many
of you that I must forgive and so I shall when I am dancing
with my tribe during the powwow at the end of the world.

EXPLORING VOCABULARY

Look up the word *powwow* in the dictionary and in an encyclopedia.
Share your findings with the class.

PROFILING ISSUES

Using the profile sheet on page 198, write a profile of the issue Alexie
describes. You may have to read between the lines—or make inferences—to address some of the categories. When you are finished, discuss
your answers with a small group of your peers or with the entire class.

EXPLORING THE TEXT

1. What is the sequence of events here?
2. Why do you think Alexie chose to write this poem in one stanza?
3. What is the theme of the poem?
4. What is the speaker's tone?

EXPLORING IDEAS

1. What do we know about the speaker?
2. To whom is the speaker referring when he or she says, " I am told
   by many of you . . ."?

3. What is the speaker being told to forgive?
4. What is forgiveness? Have you ever had to forgive someone who treated you very badly for a number of years? Was it difficult?

A Dose of Reality: The Truth about North America's Greatest Drug Problem. Ritalin (ESSAY)

RICHARD DEGRANDPRE

PREREADING

Do some research on the drug Ritalin. Consider the following questions: What does Ritalin do? Who takes it and why? What effects does it have on the body? Share your findings with the class.

ANNOTATING

While reading, underline any ideas the author sets forth that he does not appear to support. In the margins, note what kind of support would strengthen his ideas.

On any given day in North America, almost five million kids will take a powerful psychostimulant drug. The geographical caveat is important: more kids in North America are diagnosed with attention deficit disorder (ADD) and given drugs like Ritalin to "help" them behave than in the rest of the world combined. In fact, the US and Canada account for a startling 95 percent of worldwide Ritalin consumption. (1)

In the midst of this drug epidemic, April 2001 appeared to signal a backlash. Two television magazines, PBS's *Frontline* and A&E's *Investigative Reports,* pondered the massive increase in use, as did a five-part series in Canada's *National Post* newspaper. Still, of all the critical reports in recent months, none has come any closer to facing the hard facts about Ritalin than have the hundreds that came before. (2)

Fact one: While medical "experts" and the media persistently deny it, developmental studies have now established that certain differences in caregiving and family structure cause some children to become impulsive and hyperactive. In a recent example, a ten-year, federally funded study in the US, reported at the April meeting of the Society for Research in Child Development, found that the more time children spent in daycare the more unmanageable they became. Kids who spent more than 30 hours a week in daycare scored significantly higher on such things as "explosive behavior," "talking too much," "argues a lot," and "demands a lot of attention"—the very behaviors that so often lead to stimulant treatment. (3)

Fact two: Ritalin is little more than coke for kids. "Cocaine, which is one of the most reinforcing and addictive of the abused drugs, has pharmacological actions that are very similar to those of methylphenidate [Ritalin], which is the most commonly prescribed psycho-tropic medication for children in the United States." This conclusion, reported by Nora Volkow and colleagues at Brookhaven National Laboratory, appeared in the *Archives of General Psychiatry* in 1995. A follow-up study, published in the *American Journal of Psychiatry* in 1998, found that the pharmacological actions produced by oral, therapeutic doses of Ritalin were comparable to those produced by recreational doses of intranasal cocaine. Researchers are quick to point out that children prescribed Ritalin do not (usually) snort or inject it, which alters the drug-taking experience. But do we really believe parents would give their kids cocaine, even if it was only in pill form? (4)

Fact three: Ideology is driving science. Fighting the drug war, researchers like Volkow have demonstrated that continued use of cocaine and other stimulants causes brain changes. Yet never have these researchers investigated whether chronic stimulant use might produce the same effect in kids. Meanwhile, other researchers have pointed to subtle differences in certain areas of the brain to suggest that ADD is a biological disease—a claim repeated in the recent *Frontline* episode. The truth is that all these studies have looked only at hyperactive individuals who have been taking stimulants for years. At least one study, published in *Psychiatry Research* in 1986, was honest in its findings: "Since all of the [ADD] patients had been treated with stimulants, cortical atrophy [i.e., brain deterioration] may be a long-term adverse effect of this treatment." (5)

Fact four: The US Drug Enforcement Administration has long known that massive amounts of Ritalin are being diverted by adolescents and adults into recreational use, where it's often crushed up and snorted, or even injected. The DEA reported that Ritalin misuse in high schools increased from three to 16 percent from 1992 to 1995. Similarly, it found that while children between the ages of ten and 24 were involved in about 25 emergency-room visits connected with Ritalin misuse in 1991, the number had jumped to 1,725 by 1998. (6)

Fact five: Stimulants are no cure. Perhaps all this hypocrisy could be excused if stimulant "treatment" somehow worked, but it doesn't—at least not for the children themselves. Parents have been encouraged to believe that pharmacological control will boost their child's learning and social skills, but this rarely happens. Dozens of objective studies have assessed the long-term effectiveness of stimulants on children's academic performance, social development and self control. None has shown them to be effective for anything but controlling kids' behavior—an effect that vanishes once the drug wears off. Such studies rarely make the headlines, however. Instead, we hear about recent research from the US—"the MTA study"—that relied heavily on subjective reports from teachers and parents while ignoring its own objective findings, which showed little promise for drug treatment. Reporting on this research, the media too, has found a cure where there isn't one. (7)

So where does the cure lie? It lies in prevention. This means getting back to basics as a culture, with parents who have and take the time to truly matter in the lives of children. (8)

EXPLORING VOCABULARY

Define the word *ideology*. Then explain what the author means in paragraph five when he writes, "Ideology is driving science." Share your findings with the class.

PROFILING ISSUES

Using the profile sheet on page 198, write a profile of the issue DeGrandpre describes. You may have to read between the lines—or make inferences—to address some of the categories. When you are finished, discuss your answers with a small group of your peers or with the entire class.

EXPLORING THE TEXT

1. Why does the author use the phrases "Fact one," "Fact two," "Fact three," etc.? How else might he have started each of those paragraphs?
2. What is the author's purpose?
3. What is the main idea?
4. Does the author set forth any ideas that he does not support? (Review your annotations.)

EXPLORING IDEAS

1. What are the five facts that DeGrandpre sets forth?
2. Do you agree with the author's position? Why or why not?
3. What solutions does DeGrandpre offer? Can you offer any additional solutions?
4. Do you know anyone who uses—or abuses—Ritalin? What effects does the drug have on that person?

Racism and Sexism in the Media (Textbook Excerpt)

Margaret Andersen and Howard F. Taylor

PREREADING

Watch an hour of prime-time television—including commercials—and make a list of how many people you encounter of the same race, ethnicity, and gender as you. Also note the kinds of roles they play. Share your findings with the class.

ANNOTATING

While reading, underline anything in the article that seems to address what you witnessed in your research. In the margins, note whether the information reinforces or contradicts your findings.

Many sociologists have argued that the mass media promote narrow definitions of who people are and what they can be. What is considered beauty, for example, is not universal; ideals of beauty change as cultures change and depend upon what certain cultural institutions promote as beautiful. Aging is not beautiful, youth is; light skin is promoted as more beautiful than dark skin (regardless of one's race) although being "tan" is seen as more beautiful than being pale. In African American women's magazines, the models typified as most beautiful are generally those with clearly Anglo features—light skin, blue eyes, and straight or wavy hair. These depictions have fluctuated over time; in the early 1970's for example, there was a more Afrocentric ideal of beauty—darker skin, "Afro" hairdos, and African clothing. Today, images of African American women have returned to more Anglocized depictions of beauty. European facial features are also pervasive in the images of Asian and

Latino women appearing in U.S. magazines. The media communicate that only certain forms of beauty are culturally valued; these ideals are not somehow "natural"; they are constructed by those who control cultural and economic institutions (Kassell, 1995; Wolf, 1991; Barthel, 1988; Chapkis, 1986).   (1)

Images of women and racial and ethnic minorities in the media are similarly limiting. Content analyses of television reveal that during prime time, men are a large majority of the characters shown. On soap operas, women are cast either as evil or good, but naïve. One study of commercials on MTV finds that in music videos, women characters appear less frequently, have more beautiful bodies, are more physically attractive, wear more sexy and skimpy clothing, and are more often the object of another's gaze than their male counterparts (Signorielli et al., 1994).   (2)

Even though African Americans and Hispanics watch more television than Whites do, they are a small proportion of TV characters, generally confined to a narrow variety of character types, depicted in stereotypical ways. Latinos are often stereotyped as criminals or passionate lovers. African American men are most typically seen as athletes and sports commentators, criminals, or entertainers. It is difficult to find a single show where Asians are the principal characters—usually they are depicted in silent roles as domestics or other behind-the-scenes characters. More often, they are in the background as domestic workers or extras. Native Americans make occasional appearances where they usually are depicted as mystics or warriors; typically, if presented at all, Native Americans are marginal characters stereotyped as silent, exotic, and mysterious. Jewish women are generally invisible on popular TV programming, except when they are ridiculed in stereotypical roles (Kray, 1993). Class stereotypes abound, as well, with working-class men typically portrayed as being ineffectual, even buffoonish (Butsch, 1992; Dines and Humez, 1995). On television, people of color are also far more likely to be found in comedies than dramas. African American women, especially, are most typically seen as characters in comedy shows. In dramas, African Americans and Latino men are typically the sidekicks, not the major character.   (3)

Women and racial-ethnic minorities are also seriously underrepresented in and on network news, one of the most important outlets of information about society and culture. They are underrepresented as news commentators, as correspondents, as news directors, and as news subjects (Rhode, 1995; Gibbons, 1992; Ziegler and White, 1990). Although by the 1990s, women's representation among network news reporters had increased, they are only 15 percent of network news reporters and 20 percent of print journalists (though they are 68 percent of journalism school graduates). Men write two-thirds of the front-page stories in the news and provide 85 percent of television reporting; only 3 percent of newspaper executives are women. Women of color are even further underrepresented, providing only 2 percent of broadcast media stories. Men also provide 85 percent of quotes or references in the media, are 75 percent of those interviewed on TV, and are 90 percent of the most recently cited pundits—even on issues that involve women (Rhode, 1995). With limited coverage of issues important to women and racial-ethnic groups, the public can hardly be well informed about race and gender as social and political issues. This has led sociologists to conclude that the news media reflect the White male social order and primarily support the "public, business, and professional upper middle-class sectors of society" (Gans, 1979: 61). It is therefore not surprising that many minorities are dissatisfied with how they see themselves represented in the media (McAneny, 1994).   (4)

Television is not the only form of popular culture that influences public consciousness about gender and race. Music, film, books, and other industries play a significant role in molding public consciousness. What images are produced by these cultural forms? Studies of rock videos are instructive. Even with the relatively recent introduction of Black Entertainment Television (BET) and other shows focusing on Black and Latino artists, more than three-fourths of rock videos feature White male singers or bands led by White men. Rock videos more often depict White men as the center of attention; women and African American or Hispanic men are rarely shown in the foreground. Typically, White women are depicted as trying to get the attention of men; African Americans are more likely than Whites to be seen singing and dancing.   (5)

Do these images matter? In an example of the influence of popular culture on people's beliefs, researchers designed experiments to assess the influence of listening to heavy-metal rock on men's attitudes toward women. They found that exposure to heavy-metal rock music increases men's stereotyping of women, including their acceptance of violence against women, regardless of the lyrical content. This same study also found that men reported more sexual arousal from hearing "easy-listening classical music" than they did from hearing heavy-metal music! (St. Lawrence and Joyner, 1991). More than mere cultural curiosities, the artifacts and images that cultural institutions promote have an enormous effect on people's lives.

(6)

References

Barthel, Diane. 1988. *Putting on Appearances: Gender and Advertising.* Philadelphia: Temple University Press.

Butsch, Richard. 1992. "Class and Gender in Four Decades of Television Situation Comedy." *Critical Studies in Mass Communication* 9: 387–399.

Chapkis, Wendy. 1986. *Beauty Secrets: Women and the Politics of Appearance.* Boston: South End Press.

Dines, Gail, and Jean M. Humez, eds. 1995. *Gender, Race and Class in Media: A Text-Reader.* Thousand Oaks, CA: Sage Publications.

Gans, Herbert. 1979. *Deciding What's News: A Study of the CBS Evening News, NBC Nightly News, Newsweek and Time.* New York: Pantheon.

Gibbons, Sheila. 1992. *Media Report to Women* (Fall): 5–6.

Kassell, Scott. 1995. "Afrocentrism and Eurocentrism in African American Magazine Ads." Princeton, NJ. Unpublished senior thesis.

Kray, Susan. 1993. "Orientalization of an 'Almost White' Woman. The Interlocking Effects of Race, Class, Gender, and Ethnicity in American Mass Media." *Critical Studies in Mass Communication* 10 (December): 349–366.

McAneny, Leslie. 1994. "Ethnic Minorites' View of the Media's View of Them." *The Gallup Poll Monthly* (August, No. 347): 31–41.

Rhode, Deborah L. 1995. "Media Images, Feminist Issues." *Signs* 20 (Spring): 685–710.

Signorielli, Nancy, Douglas McLeod, and Elaine Healy. 1994. "Gender Stereotypes in MTV Commercials: The Beat Goes On." *Journal of Broadcasting and Electronic Media* 38 (Winter): 91–101.

St. Lawrence, Janet S., and Doris J. Joyner. 1991. "The Effects of Sexually Violent Rock Music on Males' Acceptance of Violence Against Women." *Psychology of Women Quarterly* 15: 49–63.

Wolf, Naomi. 1991. *The Beauty Myth: How Images of Beauty are Used Against Women*. New York: William Morrow and Co.

Ziegler, Dhyana, and Alisa White. 1990. "Women and Minorities on Network Television News: An Examination of Correspondents and Newsmakers." *Journal of Broadcasting and Electronic Media* 34 (Spring): 215–223.

EXPLORING VOCABULARY

Define the terms *ethnocentrism* and *patriarchy*. Then, with a small group of your classmates, see how those terms relate to the reading. Share your answers with the class.

PROFILING ISSUES

Using the profile sheet on page 198, write a profile of the issue Andersen and Taylor describe. You may have to read between the lines—or make inferences—to address some of the categories. When you are finished, discuss your answers with a small group of your peers or with the entire class.

EXPLORING THE TEXT

1. Find the topic sentences in each of the paragraphs. Does each paragraph have one?
2. What does the information in parentheses mean? Why is some of the information different?
3. What kinds of evidence do the authors offer to support their stance? Does the evidence seem reliable?
4. What is the main idea? Is it implicit or explicit?

EXPLORING IDEAS

1. Did your research reinforce or contradict the information in the article? (Review your annotations.)
2. Do the authors account for why racism and sexism exist in the media? How do you account for it?
3. What is the meaning of the term *public consciousness* as the authors use it in paragraph five?
4. If you were reading this article for a test in a sociology class, what information might show up on a test? Why?

To Pet or Not to Pet? (ESSAY)

NADYA LABI

PREREADING

Do some research on dolphins. Consider the following questions: What do they eat? In what parts of the world do they live? What is the relationship between dolphins and other sea creatures? What is the relationship between dolphins and humans? Share your findings with the class.

ANNOTATING

While reading, underline any words, phrases, or sentences that surprise or upset you. In the margins, briefly explain why.

We *Homo sapiens* are easily flattered. We like dolphins because they seem to like us. They smile—or rather, their mouths curve upward in an illusion of cheeriness—and we feel the urge to touch, to pet, to be nearer. It hardly registers that dolphins smile even when they have nothing to smile about.   (1)

Luna died smiling. The bottle-nosed dolphin was captured last December off the southwest coast of Baja California. For two hours, she traveled in a coffin-like trailer with virtually no water. When she arrived at her destination, an aquarium at La Concha Beach resort in La Paz, Mexico, she was carried in a makeshift hammock and deposited on a sandy beach. She tried to bite her handlers, but her protest went unheeded. She was forced to frolic and swim with tourists in a pen. After five weeks, she died—from stomach inflammation and ulcers caused by stress, according to the autopsy report. A leading Mexican environmental organization, the Group of One Hundred, is pressing for release of Luna's seven traveling companions. "These dolphins are overworked and in horrible conditions," says Homero

Aridjis, a poet who is the organization's president. "This is dolphin-napping."

(2)

Many tourists would be horrified at the thought. A growing number of them are getting a natural high by bonding with these seagoing mammals in aquatic parks both in and outside the U.S. In 18 national programs, visitors can pay up to $150 to hop into the pool for a half-hour "swim with" the dolphins. These U.S. programs generally treat their featured attractions well: dolphins are no longer captured in the wild, and there are guidelines to limit the mammal's workday (no more than two hours) and office space (a sanctuary away from humans is required).

(3)

But such standards are less likely to be followed in parks outside the U.S. In Cuba, the source for many of the dolphins that end up in Caribbean aquariums, a fisherman can earn more than a year's income by selling a wild dolphin on the black market for about $800. Once trained, that same dolphin can fetch $1,500 a day at a Caribbean park. Several cases have been reported of dolphins suffering from stress, chlorine toxicity or an overdose of human affection. "Dolphins don't just drop out of the sky and end up in tanks," says Gwen McKenna, an activist in Ontario, Canada, who seeks to eradicate swim-withs. "They are literally being mauled by humans all day long. These tanks are death traps for them."

(4)

At Manati Park in the Dominican Republic, one of the world's most controversial facilities, techno music blares from two large speakers as dolphins bounce balls and beach themselves on concrete for $7 photo ops. Then the contact sport begins. To the strains of a Celine Dion ballad, a girl douses her hands and feet in disinfectant and grabs hold of dolphin Vicki's pectoral fins. Vicki pulls her passenger along the length of the 10-yd by 17-yd. pool and returns to the trainer for a reward—two pieces of fish. Vicki then swims up to a group of six swimmers for some petting. The entire session costs $65. "It was a marvelous experience," said Michelle Loeffler, a dance teacher from Peoria, Ill. "But I felt bad they have only that little pool to swim in." Said another tourist: "I don't like the idea of circuses, but this seemed like a nice way to meet the dolphins."

(5)

These meet-and-greets present risks to all parties involved. Dr. Santiago Gallo, a gastroenterologist who has treated dolphins in Mexico, reports cases in which dolphins have swallowed keys, a swimming cap and even a disposable diaper. Worse, critics charge that several dolphins have died prematurely at Manati because of toxic waters. Responds Javier Moreno, the owner of Manati: "If there are deaths, this is not a surprise. There is a cycle of life. They die. They are born." He plans to expand the facility and add five dolphins to the roster next year. (6)

Humans can also face perils from these encounters. Recent data are hard to come by, since swim programs are not required to report human injuries. But a 1995 study in the U.S. found that dolphins, particularly those in unstructured swim-with programs, occasionally acted aggressively toward humans. The British-based Whale and Dolphin Conservation Society claims it has witnessed three encounters at Manati that endangered humans. (7)

Some facilities work harder than others to make dolphins feel at home. Dolphins Plus, in Key Largo, Fla., fences off an area of the Florida Bay, thereby connecting the play area to the ocean. One of its owners, Rick Borguss, also holds stock in nearby Dolphin Cove, a natural lagoon surrounded by palm trees where children with disabilities interact with sea mammals. Orlando's Discovery Cove has three man-made lagoons, seven holding pools, a medical pool for sick animals and a staff of 70-plus workers to tend to the needs of 30 dolphins. (8)

Defenders of these aquariums insist that their goal is to educate, not exploit. "There are billions of people who have no access to animals or [any way to] learn about nature," says Borguss. "People who leave here appreciate the animals." Discovery Cove produces curriculum guides and encourages its specialists to visit local schools. A federal study conducted last year appears to back up the claim that playing with people is no more harmful to the dolphins than performing for them. It found that 12 "interactive" dolphins exhibited no greater stress than their counterparts who simply took part in shows. (9)

That doesn't address a more fundamental question: Should dolphins become human pets? "I can show you a dolphin born inside of a building that has never seen the ocean, live fish or the sky," says Ric O'Barry, a consultant for the World Society for the Protection of Animals. "These are freaks we have created for our own amusement." He advises tourists not to buy tickets for dolphin swims or shows. But that flies in the face of another fact of nature—human nature. (10)

EXPLORING VOCABULARY

With a small group of your classmates, look up the prefix *aqua* on page 204 and find the words in the article that use the prefix. What do those words mean? Try to list other words that use the prefix. Share your answers with the class.

PROFILING ISSUES

Using the profile sheet on page 198, write a profile of the issue Labi describes. You may have to read between the lines—or make inferences—to address some of the categories. When you are finished, discuss your answers with a small group of your peers or with the entire class.

EXPLORING THE TEXT

1. What is the main idea?
2. What is the purpose?
3. Labi contrasts American dolphin parks with international dolphin parks. What are the differences between the two?
4. What are the similarities between the two?

EXPLORING IDEAS

1. According to the article, what are the problems with dolphin parks? What are the benefits?
2. In paragraph six, Labi quotes Javier Moreno who says, "If there are deaths, this is not a surprise. There is a cycle of life. They die. They are born." Do you agree with him? Why or why not?
3. Reread the last paragraph. What does Labi mean by the last sentence in that paragraph?
4. Have you ever been to a dophin park? If so, what was it like? If not, would you like to visit one?

SUGGESTIONS FOR READING ABOUT ISSUES

Nickled and Dimed by Barbara Ehrenreich

Amazing Grace: The Lives of Children and the Consciousness of a Nation by Jonathan Kozol

Black and Blue by Anna Quindlen

SUGGESTIONS FOR SUMMARIZING ESSAYS ABOUT ISSUES

Choose one of the following works from Unit Five and write a summary. Follow the guidelines for writing a summary on page 207.

"To Pet or Not to Pet?" by Nadya Labi

"In Praise of the F Word" by Mary Sherry

SUGGESTIONS FOR WRITING ABOUT ISSUES

1. Choose an issue that you face or have faced in your life and explain how you deal with or have dealt with it. Be sure to define the issue thoroughly.
2. Write a letter to one of the authors in this unit and disagree with his or her position. Be sure to support your own position thoroughly.
3. Visit a local community organization and interview the volunteers and employees. Write an essay about the issue they address and the ways they address it. Use the profile sheet in this unit to help you gather information about the issue.
4. Write an essay about an issue that your family is currently facing. Discuss how it is affecting your life and how you are trying to address the issue.
5. Brainstorm with some classmates about solutions to a particular issue at your school. As a group, write a letter to the editor of your school newspaper, the editor of your local newspaper, or the president of your student government organization.
6. Choose an issue in your community that you think needs immediate attention and write a letter to your congressional representative asking for help or suggesting possible solutions. Be sure to define the issue thoroughly.

7. Read one of the books listed and write an essay profiling the issue being discussed. Use the profile sheet in this unit to help you gather information about the issue.

PROFILING ISSUES

Fill in the following information about one or more of the issues you have read about in Unit Five. Remember that the information in some categories may not be directly stated; it may be implied. If it is implied, use clues given by the author to infer the answer. Remember also that the information in some categories may not be directly stated or implied, so do not just guess at any given category.

ISSUE _____

ORIGIN OR CAUSE _____

SUPPORTING POSITION _____

SUPPORTING EVIDENCE _____

SUPPORTING POPULATION _____

AGE(S) _____

LOCATION(S) _____

SOCIOECONOMIC CLASS(ES) _____

CULTURAL/PHILOSOPHICAL AFFILIATION(S) _____

DISSENTING POSITION _____

DISSENTING EVIDENCE _____

DISSENTING POPULATION _____

AGE(S) _____

LOCATION(S) _____

SOCIOECONOMIC CLASS(ES) _____

CULTURAL/PHILOSOPHICAL AFFILIATION(S) _____

MIDDLE GROUND POSITION _____

POPULATION AFFECTED _____

CONSEQUENCES TO THOSE AFFECTED _____

POSSIBLE SOLUTIONS _____

APPENDICES

Appendix I ~ Context Clues

Often when you are reading, you will come across words that you do not understand or cannot readily define. Not knowing the meaning of a word can hamper your understanding of the whole sentence or passage. It is very important, then, to do your best to know the meaning—at least an approximate meaning—of every word in your reading material. Equally true, however, is the fact that most people do not want to stop to look up the words they do not understand. Luckily, a good strategy for comprehending new words is to use *context clues*. Context clues help us discover a word's meaning by giving us the definition of the word or by giving us hints so we can adequately construct a definition ourselves.

DEFINITION CONTEXT CLUES

The definition context clue gives us the actual definition in the same sentence or in another sentence.

Example 1

The McKay team has presented four pieces of evidence in support of their claim that Mars may have supported single-celled organisms in the distant past. (1) The rock contains globules of carbonate that have a structure and chemical composition that suggest they were deposited from an *aqueous* (**water-containing**) solution.

From "Is There Life on Mars" on page 47. (Boldface added.) Here, the definition of the word *aqueous* is contained in parentheses directly after the word itself.

Example 2

Food is a fundamental requirement of all animals; no animal can survive without eating. Natural selection has therefore provided animals with mechanisms to ensure that the impulse to eat arises when nutrients are needed. In humans, however, these natural impulses, so crucial to our health and well-being, can go terribly awry. In recent decades we have seen an increase in the occurrence of *eating disorders*, **ailments characterized by the disruption of normal eating behavior.**

From "Health Watch: Eating Disorders—Betrayal of the Body on page 139.

(Boldface added.)

In this case, the definition of the term *eating disorders* is given in the same sentence immediately following the term. Instead of being inside parentheses, the definition is set off from the word with a comma.

Example 3

The young men dodge, circle, running the broken field, and suddenly stand very still as the car draws close. They are immediately added to the cold statistics of border apprehensions. But they are really mere sacrifices; over on the left, three other men run low and hunched, like infantrymen in a fire fight. "*Corre, corre,*" Jeronimo Vasquez whispers. "***Run, run.*** . . ." They do.

From "Along the Tortilla Curtain" on page 50. (Boldface added.)

In this example, the definition of *corre* is given in the next sentence.

HINT CONTEXT CLUES

The hint context clue does not define the word, but gives readers valuable hints or clues so that they can figure out the meaning themselves.

Example 1

In the following passage, the word *blight* is not deliberately defined by the author, yet there are many clues in the rest of the paragraph that help the reader understand that a blight is a sickness of some sort.

Then a **strange** *blight* crept over the area and **everything began to change.** Some evil **spell** had settled on the community: **mysterious maladies** swept the flocks of chickens; the **cattle and sheep sickened and died.** Everywhere was a **shadow of death.** The farmers spoke of **much illness** among their families. In the town the doctors had become more and more puzzled **by new kinds of sickness appearing**

among their patients. There had been **several sudden and unex-plained deaths,** not only among adults but even among children, who would be stricken suddenly while at play and die within a few hours.

From "A Fable for Tomorrow" on page 55. (Boldface added.)

Example 2

In the following sentence, the author has not given the reader a defini-tion of the word *sadism*. The author does include, however, three specific clues that help the reader understand *sadism* as finding enjoyment in causing pain.

One has but to watch the **gleam** in the eye of the holy-mouth-man, as he **jabs** an awl into an **exposed nerve**, to suspect that a certain amount of sadism is involved.

From "The Body Ritual Among the Nacirema" on page 93. (Boldface added.)

Example 3

In the following passage, the hints for the meaning of *Afrocentric* are found throughout the passage. The clues help the reader understand the word to mean things focused on African style or culture or appearance.

In African American women's magazines, the models typified as most beautiful are generally those with clearly Anglo features—light skin, blue eyes, and straight or wavy hair. These **depictions have fluctuated** over time; in the early 1970's for example, there was a more *Afrocentric* ideal of beauty—**darker skin, "Afro" hairdos,** and **African clothing.** To-day, images of African American women have returned to more Angli-cized depictions of beauty.

From "Racism and Sexism in the Media" on page 186. (Boldface added.)

Appendix II ~ Word Parts

A valuable skill to have when reading new material and encountering new words is to know the meaning of word parts: prefixes, suffixes, and roots. Then, when you encounter words you cannot define, you will be able to make an educated guess by being able to define the word parts.

COMMON PREFIXES

a	without, not	amoral
ab	away, from	abnormal
ad	toward	advance
amphi	both, around	amphibian
ante	before	antecedent
anti	against	antisocial
bene	good	beneficial
bi	two	bilingual
cent	hundred	centennial
com	with, together	communicate
de	down	detract
dec, deca	ten	decade
demi	half	demitasse
dia	through	diameter
dis	not, opposite	disappointed
ex	out, from	exhale
extra	beyond	extraordinary
hyper	above, excessive	hypersensitive
hypo	under	hypodermic
il	not	illegal
im	not	impossible
in	not	inconsiderate
inter	between	interstate
intra	within	intramural
mal	wrong	maladjusted

mill	thousand	millipede
mis	wrong, ill	misdiagnosed
mono	one	monopoly
nove	nine	November
oct	eight	October
omni	all	omniscient
poly	many	polygamous
post	after	posthumous
pre	before	prenatal
pro	for	profess
proto	first	prototype
quad	four	quadruple
re	again	reproduce
semi	half	semicircle
sex	six	sextuplets
sub	under	submarine
super	above, over	supervise
trans	across	transport
tri	three	triangle
uni	one	unicycle

COMMON WORD ROOTS

ama	love	amiable
aqua	water	aquarium
astro	star	astrology
aud	hear	audible
auto	self	autobiography
bio	life	biology
card	heart	cardiology
cosmo	universe	cosmopolitan
demos	people	democracy
dent	teeth	dentures
derma	skin	dermatology
duct	lead	conduct
gene	race, kind	geneology
grad	go	graduation
graph	write	autograph

gyn	woman	gynecology
hab	to have	habitat
homo	man	homosexual
lum	light	luminous
macro	large	macrocosm
mater	mother	maternal
manu	hand	manual
med	middle	mediate
micro	small	microcosm
mort	die	mortality
mut, muta	change	mutable
nat	to be born	nativity
neg	deny	negative
ortho	straight	orthodontist
pater	father	paternal
path	disease	pathology
ped	foot	pedestrian
phon	sound	symphony
port	carry	portable
psych	mind	psychology
quir	ask	inquire
scrib	write	prescribe
sol	alone	solitude
somnia	sleep	insomniac
soph	wisdom	philosophy
spect	look at	spectacle
tele	distant	telecommunications
theo	God	theology
therma	heat	thermal
vis	see	vision

COMMON SUFFIXES

able	able to	curable
al	characterized by	logical
ance	action, quality	resistance
ant	one who	servant
chrome	color	monochrome

cide	killing	suicide
ence	quality of	patience
er	one who	singer
fic	making	horrific
ful	full	awful
fy	form into	clarify
ible	able to	visible
ism	manner of action	racism
ite	one who	Israelite
itis	inflammation	laryngitis
ity	quality of	charity
ive	quality of	progressive
less	without	thoughtless
ment	quality of	judgment
ology	study of	criminology
or	one who	legislator
tude	degree of	solitude
wards	facing	towards
y	full of	silly

Appendix III ~ Summary Writing

A summary is a *report* of the content of an essay, an article, a short story, a movie, or any other work. Summaries do not include the opinions or beliefs of the summary writer; instead, they *report* the content of the work being summarized. Writing competent summaries is a wonderful study aid; it also is an important part of writing research papers, which you may do in this class and you will certainly do in later classes. Writing competent summaries is also a great method for learning how to read more closely and write more effectively and succinctly.

There are many ways to write a summary, but this book will teach you just one way. This type of summary is geared toward essays because it works with the standard structure of an essay: introduction, body, and conclusion.

SUMMARY STEPS

1. Read and annotate the assigned essay. While annotating, underline the main idea and the important supporting points. For practice, read "A Dose of Reality: The Truth about North America's Greatest Drug Problem. Ritalin" by Richard DeGrandpre on page 182.

2. Find the main idea of the essay, write it in your own words and include the title of the essay and the name of the author. Example: *In his essay, "A Dose of Reality: The Truth about North America's Greatest Drug Problem. Ritalin," Richard DeGrandpre contends that Ritalin is being overly prescribed by medical professionals and overly welcomed by parents who want their children to be well behaved.*

3. Read the essay again and divide it into logical parts. First, identify the introduction, the body, and the conclusion. Then look back into the body and see if there are any major topic shifts. If there are, you should divide the body into as many parts as are

necessary to represent each major topic shift. DeGrandpre's essay is easy to divide because he provides us with headings in the body of the work. The introduction consists of paragraphs one and two. The first body part consists of paragraph three (fact one); the second body part consists of paragraph four (fact two); the third body part consists of paragraph five (fact three); the fourth body part consists of paragraph six (fact four); the fifth body part consists of paragraph seven (fact five); and the conclusion consists of paragraph eight.

4. Look for the main idea or main thrust of each section. Do not rewrite each section; just put the main idea of each section into your own words. Quote only striking or important words, phrases, or sentences.

5. Write your summary in one paragraph. Begin the paragraph with the main idea of the entire selection and continue the paragraph with your summary of each section. Follow the sequence of the essay. Be sure to use transition, cite the author consistently, and vary your verb phrases.

Sample Summary of "A Dose of Reality: The Truth about North America's Greatest Drug Problem. Ritalin."

In his essay, "A Dose of Reality: The Truth about North America's Greatest Drug Problem. Ritalin," Richard DeGrandpre contends that Ritalin is being overly prescribed by medical professionals and overly welcomed by parents who want their children to be well behaved. DeGrandpre opens by sharing the news that North American children "account for a startling 95 percent of worldwide Ritalin consumption." He notes that the North American media has begun to question this excessive reliance on Ritalin, but he suggests that the media has not questioned intensely enough. DeGrandpre continues by sharing five "hard facts" about Ritalin use. First, he cites recent studies which suggest that children can become hyperactive and ill because of their family environment and not because of their brain chemistry. Second, he asserts that Ritalin has the same effect on the body as cocaine. Third, he argues that "brain deterioration" is a long-term effect of Ritalin. Fourth, he points out that Ritalin is often used as a "recreational" drug, which causes medical problems. Fifth, he states that Ritalin does not "cure" the very disorders it is meant to treat; instead, he claims the use of Ritalin simply makes life easier for parents and teachers. DeGrandpre closes by suggesting that when parents take a greater interest in their children Ritalin will not be necessary.

Appendix IV ~ Characteristics of Effective Writing

There is only one real rule in writing: "If it works, it works." Of course, such a rule does not provide much guidance to those who struggle with writing. What is helpful, however, is to understand what characteristics make writing effective.

CONTROLLING IDEA

All good writing—no matter its form—has a controlling idea or a main point. In a short story or a poem, the controlling idea is called the theme and is usually implicit (stated indirectly.) In an essay, the controlling idea can be implicit or explicit (stated directly). When the main point of an essay is directly stated, it is called a **thesis statement.**

The controlling idea—implicit or explicit—controls what ideas actually make it into an essay and what ideas do not. It states the single main point of the essay and lets the reader know what is to come. As readers, we must find the controlling idea so that we will understand the work. As writers, we must provide our readers with a clear, strong controlling idea so they can understand our work. When learning how to write, then, it is important to use explicit controlling ideas—thesis statements—so that our readers do not get confused.

Effective thesis statements share three characteristics:

1. An effective thesis statement makes a declaration.
2. An effective thesis statement is specific.
3. An effective thesis statement is demonstrable.

Example:

If you are assigned to write an essay about Mrs. Mallard, the main character in "The Story of an Hour" by Kate Chopin (page 109), you may write the following thesis statement:

While in the bedroom, Mrs. Mallard experiences a powerful physical and emotional transformation.

This thesis statement is *declarative* because it makes a firm statement; it is *specific* because it states the kind of transformation Mrs. Mallard experienced; it is *demonstrable* because it can be clearly supported with evidence from the story.

Thesis statements can appear anywhere in an essay (remember: "if it works, it works"); however, a thesis statement often works well as the last sentence of the first paragraph. When a thesis statement is placed at the end of the introduction, the introduction *leads up* to the thesis, and the rest of the essay *supports* the thesis.

Example:

In Kate Chopin's "The Story of an Hour," a young wife, Louise Mallard, learns that her husband has been killed in a train accident. Upon hearing the news, she grieves wildly and then retreats to her bedroom. Her worried sister, Josephine, implores her to come out, but Louise resists.

While in the bedroom, Mrs. Mallard experiences a powerful physical and emotional transformation.

A thesis statement like this one—located at the end of the introduction paragraph—prepares the reader for what is to come in the body of the essay.

Effective paragraphs also have controlling ideas and when they are explicit, they are called **topic sentences.** Effective topic sentences are just like effective thesis statements: They make a declaration, they are specific, and they are demonstrable.

Example:

The first signs of Mrs. Mallard's transformation are physical.

This topic sentence is effective because it makes a *declaration*, it is *specific*, and it is *demonstrable*.

Topic sentences, too, can appear anywhere in a paragraph, but a good strategy is to place your topic sentence at the beginning of the paragraph. In this way, the reader will be more likely to recognize it.

Example:

The first signs of Mrs. Mallard's transformation are physical.

When she enters her room, she feels "pressed down by a physical exhaustion that haunted her body and seemed to reach down into her soul." However, as she sits and looks out of her window, her senses expand, and she perceives her surroundings more vividly. She notices the "sounds, the scents, the color that filled the air." Her body experiences a renewal, beginning with her eyes: "The vacant stare and the look of terror that had followed it went from her eyes. They stayed keen and bright." Mrs. Mallard suffered from "heart trouble," but while in her room, her heart was rejuvenated: "Her pulses beat fast, and the coursing blood warmed and relaxed every inch of her body." Mrs. Mallard no longer feels the "physical exhaustion" she experienced when she first entered the room.

SUPPORT

Effective writing includes adequate support. A writer cannot assume that a reader will automatically be convinced of his or her point. Points must be supported, and there are many types of support used when writing essays:

Classification

Classification is a method of writing that categorizes—or classifies—a subject into subcategories or types. Writers who use this method often introduce us to the subject in a general way and then begin their classification. "Fear Not" by Jeffrey Kluger on page 142 is a good example of the use of classification.

Comparison/Contrast

When writers want to demonstrate the similarities between two or more places, ideas, people, events, etc., they use comparison. When they want to demonstrate differences between two or more subjects, they use contrast. Sometimes writers do both. In his essay, "What We Can Learn from Japan's Prisons" on page 64, James Webb contrasts the Japanese prison system with the American prison system.

Definition

Writers using definition employ the meanings of words and concepts to support a point, *or* they set forth a definition as the main point and support it. In "Dreaming: Mysterious Mental Activity at Night" on page 81, Sam Wood and Ellen Wood do both: They define dreaming, and they use definitions to do so. They employ other techniques as well.

Description

In "A Fable for Tomorrow" on page 55, Rachel Carson uses description to support her point. In other words, she appeals to the reader's five senses by setting the stage and helping him or her form a mental picture of the place about which she is writing. When writing about a place or a person or an animal—something physical and tangible—description can be very useful.

Illustration

Writers using illustration set forth a point or a thesis statement and then they support that thesis statement with examples. Robert Lake uses a great number of examples to support the point he makes about his son in "An Indian Father's Plea: Don't Label My Son a Slow Learner" on page 2.

Narration

When writers use narration, they make a point by telling a story about their lives or the lives of others. Writers generally focus on one main event and write about it in great detail; sometimes, though, they use several smaller stories to support their point. In narrative writing, the main point is often implicit—but not always. Kenny Jackson tells us the story of his last day of chemotherapy in "Reflections" on page 18.

Persuasion

Writers who want to convince a reader to believe as they do often use persuasion or argumentation. This kind of support requires a writer to take a strong position on a particular issue and then set forth reasons to support his or her position. Then each reason is supported with any of the types of support mentioned as well as statistics and testimony from experts. In the persuasive essay on page 182, "A Dose of Reality: The Truth about North America's Greatest Drug Problem. Ritalin," Richard DeGrandpre argues against the use of Ritalin. Sometimes, as is the case with "Growing Up Game" on page 104, by Brenda Peterson, the position of the writer is subtle.

Process Analysis

Illustrating the different steps involved in a certain process is what writers do when they use process analysis to support a point. Horace Miner shows us the steps of a few Nacireman rituals in the essay "The Body Ritual Among the Nacirema" on page 93.

A writing assignment will often dictate how you should support your controlling ideas, but most writings use a variety of types of support.

UNITY

Effective writing has unity, which means that everything in the paragraph or essay directly supports the controlling idea or leads up to it. The controlling idea should control the support. If it does, the paragraph or essay will have unity. If you have ever heard someone tell a story who "gets off track," you know how frustrating that can be to follow the story and/or remain interested. The same is true—perhaps even more so— with writing. A reader will have difficulty following a writer's ideas if the writer does not stay on track. If the paragraph about Mrs. Mallard's physical transformation were not unified, it might look something like this:

> *The first signs of Mrs. Mallard's transformation are physical. As she sits and looks out of her window, her senses expand, and she perceives her surroundings more vividly. She notices the "sounds, the scents, the color that filled the air." Her body experiences a renewal, beginning with her eyes: "The vacant stare and the look of terror that had followed it went from her eyes. They stayed keen and bright."* She thinks a great deal about her husband as well. There were times when she loved him and times when she did not. She feels she can be free now that he is dead.

This paragraph starts off fine, but about halfway through, the writer gets off track. The topic sentence tells us that the paragraph will be about

Mrs. Mallard's physical transformation, not her feelings about her husband.

LOGICAL ORDER

Effective writing follows a logical order. The writing assignment and the kind of support you choose will shape how you order your support.

- If you are writing a narrative essay about an important event in your life, you will probably follow a chronological order—or write about the event in the order that it happened.
- If you are writing a process analysis, you will go step by step in the appropriate sequence—or from beginning to end.
- If you are using illustration to support a point, you will probably begin with the *least* striking example of your point and lead to the *most* striking example of your point in order to build some tension.
- If you are writing a persuasive essay, you will probably begin with the least striking or convincing reason you believe what you believe and move toward the most striking or convincing reason.
- If you are writing a descriptive essay about a place, you may start with any striking landmarks and then move your way around the landscape. Or you may start at one side of the place and move toward the other.
- If you are writing an essay that compares or contrasts two subjects, you will either write about one subject then the other (subject by subject) or you will make a point about each subject, support that point, and then make another point about each subject (point by point).
- If you are writing a definition essay, you might set forth a definition of an idea or a concept and then support it with examples.

The goal here is to make sure the reader can follow your order and that the order makes sense.

TRANSITION

Effective writing "flows." In other words, in effective writing the relationship between one idea and another is clear. Also, the relationship between a supporting point and the controlling idea is clear. Transition is important within paragraphs and between paragraphs. There are many transitional devices that can be used. A good grammar handbook usually has a section discussing transition, but you have two basic choices: 1) transitional expressions and 2) transitional sentences.

Transitional Expressions

You are probably familiar with many transitional expressions; they are often used to demonstrate the relationship between ideas within paragraphs. Each expression demonstrates a specific relationship between ideas, so it is important to choose transitional expressions carefully.

Examples

also	however	next
as a consequence	in addition	nonetheless
as a result	in fact	still
finally	indeed	then
furthermore	nevertheless	therefore

Transitional Sentences

Transitional sentences serve the same function as transitional expressions: They show the relationship between ideas. Transitional sentences, however, are more often used to demonstrate the relationship between paragraphs instead of within paragraphs. Transitional sentences work by including a reference to one idea while introducing a new idea.

Examples

Not only are new parents nervous about the health of their new baby, they are nervous about their ability as parents as well.

This sentence tells us that the previous paragraph addressed the nervousness new parents feel about their baby's health and that the current paragraph will tell us how parents are nervous about their own ability.

After consulting with their pediatrician, new parents should make a first aid plan in case any serious accidents occur involving their baby.

This sentence tells us that the previous paragraph suggested that new parents should consult with their pediatrician and that the current paragraph will discuss the creation of a first aid plan.

Effective writing uses transitional expressions and transitional sentences.

CLARITY

Effective writing is clear writing. A writer can set forth the most interesting and insightful ideas ever imagined, but if the reader cannot understand them, those ideas will be lost. Consequently, it is vital that writing is clear. A logical order helps writing achieve clarity, but there are other issues to consider as well:

Grammar and Punctuation

Many readers expect writers to follow the grammar and punctuation rules consistent with standard English. Sentence structure must be sound, subjects and verbs must agree, modifiers should not dangle. Semicolons, colons, dashes, periods, commas, and apostrophes must be used correctly. It is important, then, for all writers—especially student writers—to have a good handbook as a reference when writing. It is also important for writers to take the time to learn the conventions of grammar and punctuation. The fewer mistakes a writer makes, the more likely the reader will continue reading.

Spelling

Spelling can be a real burden for many students; however, it can be an even bigger burden for the reader if it is incorrect. Misspelled words can begin to seem like a code that most readers will not care to crack. If you have difficulty spelling, now is the time to get help. Ask a friend to read over your assignments, consult with a tutor in the learning lab at your school, and review spelling rules.

Word Choice

Words are the bones of all writing, so it is important to make sure that you have chosen appropriate words to express your ideas. Do not repeat the same words over and over again. Also, avoid using words you cannot readily define. The thesaurus is a beautiful tool, but it is easily misused.

Effective writers learn how to combine all of these qualities in their work. It certainly takes practice to become an effective writer—and knowledge—but being in a writing class is the first step. You will be writing effectively before you know it.

Appendix V ~ The Writing Process

Effective writing does not happen by magic. Nor are people with great talent for writing the only people who can write effectively. The truth is that effective writing involves a great deal of planning, effort, time, and persistence—and not necessarily in that order. It is a process, not a miracle. Most effective writers engage in the following steps:

GENERATING IDEAS

Very few writers can sit down the night before an important deadline and just write the perfect essay, article, or letter. Writers usually begin the writing process by generating ideas about their topic, and there are many ways to generate ideas.

Reading and Research

A great way to generate ideas is to expose yourself to the ideas of others. Reading what others have experienced or studied or pondered is a good way to get your own juices flowing.

Free Writing

Another great way to generate ideas is free writing. When you are free writing, you just write. You do not worry about grammar or punctuation or spelling. You do not even have to write complete sentences. The point is to develop your ideas about a particular topic. You should write without stopping for at least ten minutes. That can be very difficult, but it can be done. If you run out of ideas, just write something unrelated to your topic, something like "I don't know what to write," until another idea about your topic comes to you. Believe it or not, another idea will come to you.

Brainstorming

Brainstorming is very similar to free writing, but brainstorming involves listing ideas instead of writing them out in sentence form. Again, you do not need to concern yourself with grammar, punctuation, or spelling. List your ideas for ten minutes without stopping.

SETTING GOALS

Once you have generated ideas about your topic, you must set goals that will help you achieve the characteristics of effective writing in your final work. When setting goals, you should write a working thesis statement, decide how you will support your thesis statement, and how you will organize your support. This is a good time to write an outline if outlines help you. If not, write a paragraph explaining your plan for your work.

WRITING THE FIRST DRAFT

The first draft is your first attempt to achieve the qualities of good writing. You write your complete essay: introduction, body, and conclusion. You do not have to focus too much of your writing energy on grammar, punctuation, or spelling. Your goal here is to get everything together. A first draft is very much like a dress rehearsal.

RECEIVING FEEDBACK

All writers need feedback on their work. They need to know if a reader can understand their points. A good time to get feedback on your work is after you have written your first draft because you can get some great ideas about how to improve your draft. You might consider asking a friend to read over your draft and then share his or her impressions of it, or you might get together with one of your classmates. Other options include having a conference with your instructor or visiting the writing center or learning lab on your campus. You may, in fact, want to seek feedback from more than one source.

REVISING

Once you have received feedback on your first draft, it is time to revise. The word revise means *to see again*. In the context of writing, it means to see through the eyes of your reader, to see outside of yourself. When you reach this stage of writing, you should focus on issues like whether or not your thesis statement is effective, whether or not you have enough support for your thesis statement, whether or not the order of your paragraphs and the order within your paragraphs is logical, whether or not the relationship between your ideas is clear. The revising process is like a major remodeling of your home: Big changes are made. Revision, it seems, is an ongoing process; that is, more than one revision session may be necessary.

EDITING

The editing phase of the writing process is the phase that focuses on grammar, punctuation, mechanics, spelling, and word choice. It is the phase that many student writers, unfortunately, do not take seriously enough. A well-edited work is necessary for clarity, and clarity is necessary if a reader is to understand a writer's ideas. There are several useful techniques that can help you edit your work more effectively:

1. Learn grammatical and mechanical principles.

   Knowing grammar and mechanics can help you make fewer mistakes; consequently, you will have fewer mistakes to correct in the editing phase.

2. Know your grammatical and mechanical weaknesses.

   When you know your weak areas, you can be on special lookout for them while editing your work.

3. Edit your work more than once.

   Even the most trained eye cannot find every mistake with one reading, so it is important to plan several editing sessions. You should plan these sessions a few hours—or a few days—apart because then you can see your work with fresh eyes.

4. Have someone else read your work and point out errors.

   After writing and revising, most writers have difficulty approaching their work with real objectivity. Getting someone else to read your work is a good strategy because that person may find glaring mistakes that you just did not see because you have been looking at your work for so long.

5. Use spell check.

   Most computer software includes a spell check program that can help you find your spelling mistakes and typographical errors. Of course, if you have real problems with spelling, spell check may not help you because you may not be able to choose the proper word from the options that spell check provides when it finds a misspelled word. However, most people benefit from using this tool.

6. Read your work aloud.

Few students enjoy reading their writing aloud, but it is an invaluable strategy for finding mistakes. It is also invaluable in finding problems with word choice. When we write, we have an impression of how our work sounds. When we read our work aloud, we can immediately recognize any disparities in how our work sounds and how we think it should sound.

7. Edit your work one sentence at a time.

If you edit your writing one sentence at a time, you are less likely to get caught up in the content of your work and more likely to find mistakes. You can cover up all the sentences in your work except for the sentence you are editing and/or you can examine the sentences from the last sentence to the first.

As you can see, writing effectively requires a great deal of time, focus, and effort—but it's worth it to complete a project and know that you have done your best. The process discussed here can help you complete your projects with pride.

CREDITS

Robert Lake "An Indian Father's Plea: Don't Label My Son a 'Slow Learner'" by Robert Lake, *Twin Light Trail,* No. 8. Reprinted by permission of American Indian Review, UK.

Isao Matsuo "Cherry Blossoms Glisten as They Open and Fall" by Isao Matsuo from THE DIVINE WIND: Japan's Kamikaze Force in WWII by Rikihei Inoguchi & Tadashi Nakajima. Copyright © 1958. Reprinted by permission of Naval Institute Press.

James McBride "The New Testament" from THE COLOR OF WATER by James McBride. Copyright © 1996 by James McBride. Reprinted by permission of Riverhead Books, a division of Penguin Putnam, Inc.

Patrick McMahon "Taunting of a Suicidal Woman Shocks Seattle" by Patrick McMahon, *USA TODAY,* August 30, 2001. Copyright © 2001 by USA TODAY. Reprinted by permission of USA TODAY.

Horace Miner "Body Ritual Among the Nacirema" by Horace Miner, *American Anthropologist,* 1956.

Jo Goodwin Parker "What is Poverty?" by Jo Goodwin Parker in AMERICA'S OTHER CHILDREN: Public Schools Outside Suburbia by George Henderson. Copyright © 1971 by University of Oklahoma Press. Reprinted by permission of University of Oklahoma Press.

Brenda Peterson "Growing Up" from LIVING BY WATER: True Stories of nature and Spirit by Brenda Peterson. Published by Alaska Northwest, 1990. Reissued by Fulcrum Press, September 2002. B. Peterson is a native writer and novelist, author of 13 books, including BUILD ME AN ARK: A Life with Animals and the Sequel to LIVING BY WATER, SIGNING TO THE SOUND: Vision of Nature, Animals and Spirit.

Edgar Allen Poe "The Tell-Tale Heart" by Edgar Allan Poe.

Helen Prejean Excerpt from Ch. 2 of DEAD MAN WALKING by Helen Prejean. Copyright © 1993 by Helen Prejean. Reprinted by permission of Random House, Inc.

Cheryl Saba "Familiar Footing" by Cheryl Saba

Dennis Sampson "Looking Up at Something" from CONSTANT LONGING by Dennis Sampson. Copyright © 2000 by Dennis Sampson. Reprinted by permission of Carnegie Mellon University Press.

Mary Sherry "In Praise of the 'F' Word" by Mary Sherry in *Newsweek,* July 12, 1999. Copyright © 1999 by Newsweek. Reprinted by permission. All rights reserved.

Louis Simpson "In the Suburbs" from COLLECTED POEMS by Louis Simpson. Copyright © 1990 by Louis Simpson. Reprinted by permission of Louis Simpson.

Andy Steiner "Childless . . . with Children" by Andy Steiner, *The Utne Reader,* February 2001. Reprinted by permission of Andy Steiner, Senior Editor of Utne Reader Magazine.

Anastasia Toufexis "The Right Chemistry" by Anastasia Toufexis from *Time,* February 15, 1993. Copyright © 1993 by Time, Inc. Reprinted by permission.

James Webb "What We Can Learn from Japan's Prisons" by James Webb. Reprinted by permission of Sterling Lord Literistic.

Margo Williams "Po Folks: Off with Their Heads" by Margo Williams

Samuel E. Wood and Ellen Green Wood Pp. 125-128, "Dreaming: Mysterious Mental Activity During Sleep" from THE WORLD OF PSYCHOLOGY, 3rd ed. by Samuel E. Wood and Ellen Green Wood. Copyright © 1999 by Allyn & Bacon. Reprinted by permission of Allyn & Bacon.